ASETIAN
BIBLE

ASETIAN BIBLE

KEMETIC ORDER OF ASET KA

ASETIAN MYSTERIES, VAMPIRIC MAGICK
AND PREDATORY SPIRITUALITY

LUIS MARQUES

Asetian Bible ~ First Edition

Luis Marques

Metaphysical development, past-life work, Asetian history research, validation and revision by Elënya Nefer, Luis Marques and Tânia Fonseca.

Advanced spiritual work by Elënya Nefer and Luis Marques.

Graphics and artwork by André Caetano, João Gonçalves and Tânia Fonseca.

Cover concept by Luis Marques. Cover design by André Caetano.

ASETKA

Published and edited in Portugal by Aset Ka

Apartado 52230

4202-803 Porto, Portugal

To contact the author, mail can be sent to the publisher's address using the author's name, as recipient, and the contents will be forwarded. The Aset Ka will not guarantee that every letter written to the author will be answered, but all will be forwarded.

Internal Edition published in 2007.

First Edition published in 2008.

ISBN 978-989-95694-0-9

Kemetic Order of Aset Ka

www.asetka.org   public@asetka.org

May the Serpent kiss the infinite of Her cold beauty.

~ CONTENTS ~

ASETIAN BIBLE

PART ONE

ASETIAN MYSTERIES ~ SACRED THEOLOGY

PART TWO
METAPHYSICS ~ VIBRATIONAL MAGICK

APPENDICES

Disclaimer

Asetians are by no means beings of goodness and kindness. They usually are not social, do not have any inborn friendliness over mankind and are, in fact, not very kind to people. Their spirituality is built upon predatory occultism, dark arts and secrets long forgotten to mankind. However, this does not mean that an Asetian mind is something you should fearfully run away from. It is a society that defends evolution, self-development, fights stagnation and weakness. They, above all, defend knowledge, loyalty and valor.

But, is it dangerous to study Asetian knowledge?

For the ignorant-minded, the immature beings, the obsessive, the compulsive, paranoid or ego-centered; for the weak, the numb and the slow; for those who do not question themselves over and over for the mystical facts in life and in their own past; for those who believe in religion out of everything that is pushed down their throats; for the disrespectful and arrogant towards everything that they do not know and fear; for all these people, yes, the Asetian spirituality was and will always be, a very dangerous subject to study or get involved with.

At last, the point is, no Asetian will be held responsible for what use is made with the information provided within their own works, texts and practices. This book was designed for Asetians. Those who are not one are welcome to read, meditate and question about this work. Just keep an open and sharp mind.

Welcome to our world...

INTRODUCTION

E m Hotep.
The book you are holding within your hands gathers information – spiritual, metaphysical and philosophical – whose essence was kept secret for thousands of years...

For a very long time, Aset Ka has kept secret within its walls a deep and profound spiritual tradition, which grew and developed from a dark predatory path old as time itself. The *Asetian Bible* constitutes a small grimoire of a Kemetic (Egyptian) religious tradition, metaphysical knowledge, energy techniques, concepts and actually living style, which is followed by the Asetians. Within this book will be described a path built upon predatory spirituality, where vital life force is drawn from living beings to fuel magickal abilities, energy mastery and to maintain one's personal energy system balanced.

Some of you might find these actions, workings and techniques to be inhumane, unethical or something worse, so please keep in mind that this tradition is at the edge of a dark path indeed. And while darkness does not mean harm and unbalance, it does mean secret, silent, meditative and not easily understood philosophies. A dark path is not for the masses, nor even to everyone that willingly chooses it. Darkness is a path that only the aware, the evolved and the dedicated can truly embrace.

For those who might wonder about the name of this work, *bible* is a word commonly translated simply as book and is particularly used to represent central texts of a spiritual tradition or religion. The term comes from the Latin, derived from the word *biblia*, that finds its roots in *byblos*, a term for Egyptian papyrus.

This bible is organized into two different parts: a spiritual one, and a metaphysical centered module.

The first part, which addresses different aspects of the Asetian theology, spirituality and philosophy, is strictly Asetian in nature, so most of the concepts and definitions won't really apply to everyone. This first part of the book actually wanders around very complex subjects, some of which are very subjective. As such, this part is not intended to be read lightly or in a sportive manner, as within its contents there is much symbolical information, intentionally disguised, together with some subliminal details specifically designed to the identification and pre-awakening within the Asetian family.

In the second part of the book you will find a manual of metaphysics and energy manipulation, approached as vibrational magick, which unlike the first part has many information that can be applied not only to Asetians, but also to a large spectrum of beings and scholars. This section is organized in six very distinctive chapters, that range from basic concepts of subtle energy, passing through the study of vampiric subtle anatomy, to more advanced energy manipulation and feeding techniques.

This second part of the bible was intended to be a small, direct and concise tool for Asetians, as for those interested in energy manipulation or vampirism. It is not the intention of this section to teach anyone how to master energy manipulation, nor is it to be used as definitive occult formation. It is a reference that can be easily consulted, accessed and addressed at any needed time. So, I hope that you can take something out of it, even if you are not an Asetian nor identify with the Asetian tradition.

In this section, basic steps on energy manipulation are not going to be included. It is assumed that the reader has some knowledge on energy work and practice with energy sensing. In the vampire-specific topics, some concepts and notions about vampiric practices, techniques and workings are considered a pre-requisite. Feeding types are going to be described and defined as concepts, but in-depth information on the techniques being analyzed is not going to be fully developed. This section is not a book on procedures, but a framework of concepts. One of the intentions of this work is to provide a reference source-book for Asetian vampires and otherkin that identify with the Asetian practices and vampiric tradition, in this way establishing a framework that can be applied as a default in debates about vampirism, and particularly, Asetianism.

Also to note that in this work are not included the full Asetian mysteries, which are mostly internal of the Aset Ka Order, nor will be presented the practices of Asetian high magick, ritual work and meditation. All of this knowledge is something that is slowly discovered and developed as the initiate evolves and progresses within the Asetian tradition and its own personal path. Along the text there are some intentional gaps and flaws that could be seen as misconceptions by unaware eyes, which in fact are not. They are intentionally positioned and work as another of our methods of validation and test. Keep in mind that this book is more than a mere text on the occult; it is in fact a powerful metaphysical tool. Simplification on some concepts and philosophies is strategic, since the Asetianism will remain an elitist and secretive tradition of mysteries, with a profound and unknown spirituality underlying the basic framework. With this in mind, the Asetian Bible accomplishes two things, giving the more general public, researchers and scholars, the basics and concepts on the foundation and mysteries of the dark tradition from Kemet, while leaving the Asetians and followers of the path with a solid reference on the Asetianism, opening doors for a more profound development and understanding of the inner mysteries along with their own evolution.

The concepts and practices presented in this work are valid for Asetians, and when using them to explain procedures and situations in a non-Asetian environment some factors should be taken into consideration. While some of these principles can be applied to general metaphysics, it still is Asetian-based knowledge. It does not make any sense for an individual to state that some of these things are not entirely correct because he is a vampire or energy worker and it does not work in this way for him or from his personal experience. Well, it would be like a Catholic priest insisting with a Buddhist monk that his techniques on meditation are wrong. It simply doesn't make any sense.

Another relevant information to be stated is that the Aset Ka is not a closed shell of information. It studies a wide range of knowledge and mystical traditions developed across the millennia. The whole traditions that are subject of study inside the Order belong to a large variety of knowledge inside the occult spectrum, ranging from the modern Aleister Crowley's Thelema, to ancient Oriental traditions, European traditional witchcraft, Persian, Babylonian and Sumerian sorcery, Cabalistic workings, particularly from a Qlippothic perspective, and other Left-Hand traditions like Luciferianism, ritual and astral vampirism, among many others. Asetianism has its very own identity, but its followers study many forms of art and knowledge as an aid in their personal evolution, which does not mean that they can be intertwined in a practical way. Many represent incompatible material, whose study does not mean acceptance, but simply a tool to achieve a higher gnosis.

Please keep in mind that this is not by any means a final work. The Asetian Bible reflects the true dynamic nature of the Asetians, with their empathy towards evolution and *Kheperu* – transformation in Egyptian. So while this is the first edition of the bible going to the public, it will eventually change over time, when new discoveries are made, methods evolve and adapt, more past-life work is achieved and new sections are written and added to this work. Also if the Aset Ka chooses to reveal more of the Asetian mysteries, that will be reflected in newer versions of this bible. This means that when sufficient more material is added or significant changes are needed within the contents of these texts, new versions will be released. Even though the Asetian tradition is something with such ancient roots, it is not something static and stagnated, but something that is in constant evolution, like the Asetian vampire himself. This dynamic nature of the Asetian tradition and spirituality is even expressed in some of the Kemetic Temples, like the ones from ancient Thebes that still linger today in Luxor and Karnak, where their historical growth, development and architecture expresses precisely the dynamics of the Asetian evolution. Many of these dynamics are found expressed throughout most of the Ancient Egyptian constructions, whose foundations are usually far older than the buildings found nowadays standing, because of the permanent and constant reconstruction of the temples, to progress along with the stellar alignment, metaphysical development and spiritual evolution of the soul. Being the temples living entities of energy and power, just like the very soul of the Asetians, they were in constant evolution.

Finally, others and myself, related with this work and the Order of Aset Ka, are perfectly aware that the publication of this book is going to be polemic, by its contents and approach, touching on some subjects that nowadays are still considered taboo inside the occult society. There will be criticism, from both people inside the occult scene and outside of it. And, of course, people with negative comments towards all of us will manifest, even from the ones without the wrong generalized idea of vampirism and Asetianism. All I want to state regarding this matter is that I consider it a good thing and it pleases me. I expect and look forward to those critical remarks and comments. If someone will be criticizing our philosophies, beliefs, practices or any other thing related with our own nature, life and metaphysical approach, it is because in some way they feel affected by us. Or else they wouldn't be spending their own energies attacking someone they probably don't even know and that surely would never feel attacked or intimidated by them. So, in this way, and often unconsciously, they are changed by us. We made them move and act just because of what we are and represent. That is our chaotic nature. We are catalysts of change.

The more everyone condemn and criticize the Aset Ka, the more power and self-confidence the Asetians can achieve. Asetians are the true *Adversaries*, the *Nemesis* of the vulgar stagnated society. And the antagonists want that opposition and challenge, actually *feeding* from it.

Many will not understand what is being accomplished with this book, while some might see a glimpse behind the veil of what is being presented here. But actually very few will truly understand the great picture behind it.

Most of the concepts presented in this book were already available to a more secretive part of the community and members of the Aset Ka, but now available here in a revamped format of the previous texts and a sometimes shortened, other times extended version of the Asetian Bible, especially adapted and conceived to general public access.

I hope this journey you are beginning through this book will be as enriching as mine was researching and writing it. This work was written, developed and compiled between two very different geographic locations, but both very important to me and to the Order of Aset Ka. Those places are Portugal, most importantly the city of Porto; and Egypt, the sacred lands of Ancient Kemet, where I have also been developing this work, not only in terms of direct writing, but also in metaphysical work, automatic writing and meditation. This year, when back in the ancient lands of the Asetian Empire, much spiritual work for the completeness of this book has been done in sacred locations of the Asetians. Within the walls of the mighty temples of Karnak and Luxor, below the lingering ceiling of the Horus Temple in Edfu, among the desert and remains of the remarkable Deir-el-Bahari, under the starry nights of the sacred island of Philae by the presence of Orion and Sirius in the sky, in meditations in the plateau of Giza and inside the very initiatory rooms of the King's Chamber in Khufu and Khafre Pyramids, and of course while sailing the Nile through wild Egypt under the pale moonlight, as we did countless times in the old days. It was a long odyssey, the development of this work that you are holding in your hands, not only to myself but also to the others that worked with me during this process, that is far longer than most people would think, even the ones closer to us. The planning for the release of this book is quite ancient, and has been a great process of development, research and intense metaphysical work. More than just the writing and redesign of some already existent inner texts to be ready for a presentation to the general public, the work behind which content could be disclosed and what knowledge should be kept secret was a considerably hard task. The choice of not to include practical techniques within this work became quite obvious from an initial stage. The dangers of a public release of such knowledge and the chance for it to reach unworthy hands, allied to the possibility of the inner mysteries becoming easily unveiled by the initiates, instead of the traditional discovery and evolution through the initiatory journey of the soul, was never an option for this project.

Concerning the author, I wouldn't classify myself as just an occultist, since I am also a scientist, on the traditional and scholar side of it. So, I can say that something seen from my point of view will reflect precisely that, not only a metaphysical approach, but also a practical and analytical one. Personally, I defend that science and the occult have much to learn from each other. It is somewhat recent that the occult studies became more deeply pushed away from modern science. But like for the advanced Egyptian mind... it is all entwined.

At last, but central to everything that this work represents: this is a gift from Aset to Her Children. She is the One reason for this Asetian undertaking. Her words, blessing and guidance are the true core behind this book. So cherish it, the same as we do, because it has the true essence of Aset imprinted on its subtle echoes, vibrations and feel. She is the beginning, and has no end...

May the Ka be with your Ba.

Luis Marques
Kemetic Order of Aset Ka
2007

ASETIAN BIBLE

THE TEACHINGS OF ASET

PART ONE

ASETIAN MYSTERIES
SACRED THEOLOGY

SACRED PILLARS
THE SEVEN FRAMEWORKS

The sacred pillars are a deep and vital part of the Asetian tradition. They will be represented within this work only in a pictorial form, as Ancient Egyptian symbols, since all the meanings, complexity and correlations between them will be unveiled by the slow initiatory evolution of the Asetian soul. These seven frameworks inside the Asetian religion are also magickal seals, true metaphysical *sigils* that manifest the Asetian inner world and express the workings of nature itself. They are the engines behind everything, secret keys of thought, a glimpse of the divine nature inside every Asetian. The pillars can be seen as metaphysical tools in aid to the practitioner, as archetypes in philosophical thought or as true dynamic and living entities that interact constantly in an eternal flow of time.

Ankh
Immortality

Khepri

Transformation

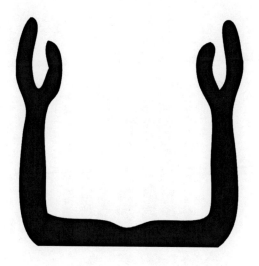

Ka
Energy

Tiet

Blood of Aset

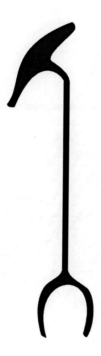

Was

Power

Ba

Soul

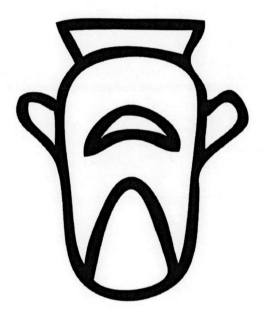

Ib

Heart

BOOK OF NUN
THE ASETIAN COSMOGONY

C osmogony is the name used to describe any philosophical theory concerning the beginning of times, the origins of the universe and the beliefs behind it. The word has its roots in the Greek *Kosmogonia*, meaning *the world to be born*.

The text within the Book of Nun is part of the Asetian sacred theology and refers to its currently accepted cosmogony.

Even though this text is mainly Kemetic in its nature, it does not reflect all the aspects and synchronisms of the Ancient Egyptian religion, that besides its complexity, symbolic nature and profound philosophical dogma, was a religion of the common people, that was eventually changed over the millennia by man, resulting in the modernly accepted Egyptian mythology, that although highly connected and entwined with the Asetian tradition, does not preserve its purity in essence and content. It is not the intention behind this work to represent a text from an Egyptologist's perspective, but the secret religious truth of the Asetians. Even though Kemetic in its basics, this cosmogony is most of all Asetian, so while many of the concepts are indeed applicable to a Kemetic religious context, they are ultimately based on an Asetian point of view. All the words presented in this work are not supposed to be a mythology background for a modern religious practice, nor a replacement for the scholarly accepted Ancient Egyptian mythology, but a metaphysical history of a divine bloodline, with its roots in the sacred lands of Kemet.

In the Book of Nun is explained, in a very short and concise way, the beginning of times, the birth of the first Gods and their rule on Earth during the Sep Tepy period. It is also described the genesis of the first-born Asetians, along with the true origins of the Gods and their history. This text touches, in tiny drops, the long-kept secret Asetian mythology. It does not address the whole complexity of the subject, nor is that the intention of this version of the Book of Nun, here made accessible to the general public for the first time. The full mysteries of the Book of Nun are a compendium of highly deep and intense religious knowledge, where some information is kept hidden inside the mind of the Asetian Elders and in the ethereal realms of the Akashic records.

The Beginning

In the beginning only existed one world, known by the ancients as *Duat*, the Underworld. Not physical, the ethereal reality was filled with nothingness and chaos. In here there was no concept of time or space. It is the infinite, the void and the abyss. With no beginning and no end. Eternal.

First, there was Nun. The abyssal waters of chaos. Unformed and unaware. Nun is the nothing that resides in the Duat, from where everything emerges. It is the never-ending cycle of the Ouroboros, forever biting its tail. Eternal death and rebirth.

From unbalances and fusion of opposites, the chaos was set in motion, and from its nothingness the primeval consciousness emerged - Amon. The primordial entity, not really a he or a she. Alone. Formed but unaware. Only Amon, known by some as Atum, existed above the nothingness of Nun. He was the demiurge, responsible for the creation of the Physical Universe.

At this point there was no past, present or future. Everything was darkness and no notion of time was yet conceived. Alone, Amon set motion for the first time, and creation was made. Splitting in two, the masculine and feminine principles emerged. The Yin and Yang of the universal essence. The male energy was practical and mind-centered, and become known as

Shu, the God of Space. The female energy was emotional and passionate, and become known as Tefnut, Goddess of Moisture.

With these two poles of divine manifestation, Amon created the physical world. As an inner shell inside the Duat, the Universe was a conceptual matrix that obeyed to physical rules, unlike the ethereal infinity of the Duat. Shu filled this whole new world with his essence, and Tefnut inhabited little spaces pulsing within it.

"Hail Atum - who made the sky.
Who created that which exists.
Lord of all that is.
Who gave birth to the Gods."
- Egyptian Book of the Dead

At this point, from the unstable energies of Amon, new forms started to emerge and gain life. The three major principals of the physical world: Maat, Goddess of Order and Balance; Khepri, God of Transformation and Rebirth; and Apophis, Daemon of Chaos and Destruction. These three concepts set in motion the whole Universe, and everywhere matter was being created and life was being seen.

Creation of Sky and Earth

Shu and Tefnut, the elder Gods of the Physical Universe, wanted to give this new world of life something special out of their own essence, and so their two children were born: Nut, the Sky; and Geb, the Earth.

The Sky had feminine energy, the beautiful and ethereal body of heavens. She became the infinite space above. The Earth had male energy. Physical, defined and strong. The foundations of physical life below.

Geb and Nut were two divine lovers. Forever present, watching over each other until the end of days, but forever apart, just touching the body of the other in a glimpse at dusk and dawn. That eternal condemnation of their

existence in the physical world is forever manifested in the feelings of the
Asetians, having them as their divine ancestors, always sensing a rush of
emotion in these portions of the day. What mattered to Geb, also mattered
to Nut. They are one, but separated... *As Above, So Below.*

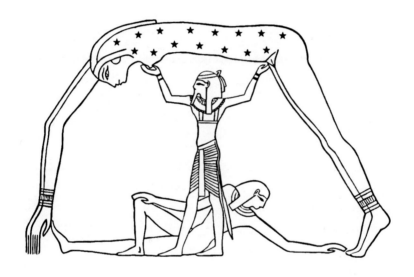

This new world was being populated with forms of life, the whole
Universe was now filled with stars and planets, and life was evolving on
Earth, from the first cells to the more complex beings. Time was being their
evolutionary catalyst. The Gods wanted to infuse life on Earth with
spiritual souls, so there would be more to the existence of these beings than
just the life they could experience on this physical realm. And so they
created the cycle of incarnations, so there could be death but also rebirth,
and in each human being a mortal Ba was incarnated, that Amon made out
of tiny water drops from the ocean of Nun. But from all this newborn life,
two particular creations were forever bound to Geb and Nut. They were the
Gods Ra and Thoth, the Sun and the Moon. Ra was bright, hot and full of
life. Thoth was dark, cold and full of knowledge.

"He fashioned mankind and engendered the Gods.
All live by that which emanated from him.
His manifestations are hidden among people.
They constitute all beings, since the time of the Gods."

- Temple of Khnum

Four Rulers of Egypt

In this creational big bang, the nothingness was moving, chaos was spreading and life was starting to flourish. As cells multiplied and life expanded in the body of Geb, the Earth, he and Nut soon had united both of their essences and created the four divine forces that would rule this Earth, such a special and beautiful place in the magnitude of the whole Physical Universe of Shu and Tefnut. And so the four magnum deities came to existence, the inheritors of divine power of the Old Gods, the essences of infinity and immortality, the foundations of past, present and future. Their names were hidden from mankind, but they became later known as Isis, Osiris, Nephthys and Seth. For the ancients, Isis sacred name was Aset.

Soon, the four Gods fell in love with the splendor of the Earth, and decided to make it their own home. They chose a sacred land, in the shores of a great river. Called it Kemet, meaning Black Land, later to be known as Egypt...

Sep Tepy

During the primordial times of this period, the Gods lived together and in harmony with the humans inhabiting the Earth, teaching them medicine, science, engineering, architecture, philosophy, writing, arts and magick. Temples were created and raised in honor of these powerful beings that never aged; priests and priestesses devoted their lives to serve them, learning their abilities and teachings.

Osiris, the primordial divine Pharaoh, ruled Egypt with his sacred wife Isis, while their brothers, Seth and Nephthys, had dominion over the sands of the desert and the beasts in the Nile. From the dark essence of Nephthys and the protector essence of Osiris, a new God emerged – the jackal Anubis. Anpu took charge of the Duat, the Underworld and ethereal reality, being the Lord of the Dead, while the other Gods kept their rule on the Physical Universe.

During this Age of the Gods, Ra was viewed as one of the leaders of the Gods Empire. Very respected, with immense power that was symbolically connected to his *secret name* that no one knew.

One day, Aset, being a master of magick and deceit, spiritually poisoned Ra and demanded his *secret name* in the exchange of Her vital magickal cure. Realizing his own powerless condition in the face of Aset's astonishing abilities, he obliged to Her demands. Being victorious in a confrontation with the mighty Ra, and by that gaining access to his terrible powers, which added to Aset's already formidable abilities, from now on Herself became the Goddess of All Gods, with supreme power over their Empire.

This occurrence alone would echo throughout eternity in a never-ending dispute from Her brother Seth and his followers, which would never accept Aset's dominion and always challenge Herself, Her children and Her followers, in an Epic Battle for Her divine throne.

> *"One falls down with terror if his ineffable name is spoken.*
> *Not even another God can call him by it.*
> *He, whose name is hidden.*
> *Because of this he is a mystery."*
>
> - Ancient Egyptian Papyrus

Isis kept rule of the worlds, while Her husband Osiris remained King of Egypt, the sacred land of the Gods on Earth. Divine protection of the Empire was ever ensured by Aset, who despite Her mighty powers, was ever closely watched by the *Seven Scorpions*, disembodied daemons bound to

Her will and life force. Servitors of the Asetian Queen, personified by the entity Serket, the scorpion leader.

Birth of the Asetians

It was during this time that Aset, being Herself a Goddess and able to move between the two worlds, the physical and the ethereal, created three souls in the Duat, out of Her purest essence.

"May your flesh be born to life.
And may your life encompass more,
Than the life of the stars as they exist."
- Pyramid Texts

These three divine Ba that emerged from the breathing of Aset were Her sacred children, integral part of Herself. She sent them to the physical world, to inhabit Geb, the Earth, on the sacred land of Kemet. Together with their holy mother, they would be able to live and experience the whole beautifulness of the physical plane. And so by the powers of Aset, these three souls were able to incarnate in the realms of the living. Aset gave birth to three children – triplets, a boy and two girls – but the world would only remember the name of Her first-born: Horus, destined to inherit Gods' kingdom on Earth – Egypt. His name would linger on, in the history of the ages, and the humans would pass on his story, tell it to their children and change it, mixing his origins and tales with other Gods, in the complexity of the Egyptian religious syncretisms, creating legends and myths of his deeds and life. But for Aset the three were one, no one better than the other, and all ultimately part of Her.

In secret, She strived for the sacred development of Her divine children, teaching them many mysteries and magick. When She felt that they were ready, She kissed them tenderly, and with Her holy hands empowered them with Her living Ka.

"She uttered the spell with the magical power of Her mouth.
Her tongue was perfect, and it never halted at a word.
Beneficent in command and word was Aset,
The one of magical spells."

— Egyptian Book of the Dead

Although divine in essence and bearers of an immortal soul, Her children were connected to the cycles of reincarnation, and did not possess the eternal physical youth of Her mother and the other elder Gods. Their body decayed and died, just like the one of a human. But their souls would endure forever.

Having a different soul and essence from all the other incarnated beings, that would manifest not only by powerful metaphysical abilities, as by an undeniable need of vital force empowerment, to sustain their high-demanding divine energy systems while incarnated in a physical shell and to fuel their developed magickal abilities and powers. That characteristic alone would earn them, thousands of years later, the denomination of *vampires…*

These *demigods* were not human, but were not so different from them either, and unlike their mother, they would not to leave the physical realm at the end of the Sep Tepy. And so they would remain here, as their own mother's representatives, always evolving, forever changing and adapting to the new realities, as societies change and shift. They soon gathered followers and allies, to which they passed knowledge and transformed their Ba, like the *sacred kiss* that Aset once gave to them, long time before, and in this way giving birth to a whole new spiritual race in the shadows of this world. They would be known as the Asetians.

To their secret and silent group Aset called *Aset Ka*, as a direct symbol of their true origins – the *Essence of Isis*, the Ka of Aset. And so She said and marked in blood, that those loyal to Her, would be forever loyal to them, because they were one. In Her *Dark Kiss* She engraved Her holy sigil deep in their very souls, that would forever be their *Asetian Mark*, and they would do the same to their followers.

"I have come that I may be your magical protection.
I give breath to your nose.
Even the North wind that came forth from Atum to your nose.
I have caused that you exist as a God.
Your enemies have fallen under your sandals.
You have been vindicated in the sky,
So that your limbs might be powerful among the Gods."
- Egyptian Book of the Dead

The three Asetians were a very united triad, a sacred and eternal metaphysical royal family. The humans used to call their company the *House of Horus*, loyal followers of the Asetian holy trinity. Inheritors of Gods' powers on Earth and leaders of the metaphysical realms of Kemet, they ruled with honor and were mostly respected by all.

End of the Gods' Rule on Earth

The fights between opposites increased on Earth, the chaotic influences augmented and the strikes of Seth unto the Asetians for the leadership of the Asetian Empire and throne of Kemet became more violent. One day, in a great metaphysical battle, Seth's increasing powers succeeded at destroying Osiris' physical body. Isis used Her breath of life to revive Osiris, but the Pharaoh was too tired of all these disputes over power. Accepting his will, Isis granted Osiris safe passage into the realm of the Duat, where he would render Anubis as the new Lord of the Dead. Osiris left Egypt never to return, and Anubis, after crowning him in his place in the realm of the dead, became the Protector of the Dead and *Keeper of the Asetians*.

> *"If I live or pass on, I am Osiris.*
> *I enter you and appear through you.*
> *I decay in you and I spring forth from you.*
> *I descend in you and I repose on your side.*
> *The Gods are living in me.*
> *As I live and grow in the emmer that sustains the exalted ones."*
>
> - Coffin Texts

Aset endured on Earth until Her children were strong enough to assume leadership of Her beloved Aset Ka, and guide the Asetians forever. Seth's attitudes condemned himself to haunt the arid and dead sands of the desert, but his battles would forever echo in eternity. His *Sethian* followers increased, and his armies fought the Aset Ka for centuries in a series of great battles that would be known as *Epic Wars*. An old scar in the face of Aset Ka that would be seen reflected in myth and lore as the battles where Seth took out *The Eye* from Horus himself. The brutality of the Sethian armies and the severity of their attacks were answered in a decisive reply from the Asetian Empire with the use of the most powerful and feared metaphysical force the world has ever seen – the *Imperial Guard* – the elite forces of the Aset Ka. Those were the darker times in history, an era of suffering, bloodshed, strive and torture.

Aset left this physical world, and kept watch of Her long gone children from afar, but never truly leaving them, because they are the Asetians... the Children of Aset.

> *"Aset will embrace you in peace.*
> *She will drive away the opponent from your path.*
> *Place your face to the West, that you may illumine the Two Lands.*
> *The dead have stood up to look at you.*
> *Breathing the air and seeing your face.*
> *Like the rising of the Sun disk in its horizon.*
> *Their hearts are pleased with what you have done.*
> *To you belong eternity and everlastingness.*
>
> - Egyptian Book of the Dead

For many years after the age of the Epic Wars, peace and beautifulness ruled the sacred lands of Kemet, until the Asetians felt there was time to fall into the mist, leaving the physical control of the lands to the human kind, and erasing the secret bloodline of the Gods from their known history. From now on living into darkness, forever watching, evolving, adapting... and living the immortality of their own kin. They became old forgotten tales in the unaware mind of the human kind, who would tell stories about them to their children and so forth, keeping their old memories alive along with their dreams, in the form of the beautiful Egyptian mythology.

The Asetian Empire would linger on in the shadows of this world, silently and in secret... and so it ended, the Kingdom of the Gods on Earth, and the human era began.

> *"Infinite time, without beginning and without end.*
> *That is what has been given to me.*
> *I inherit eternity and everlastingness."*
>
> - Egyptian Book of the Dead

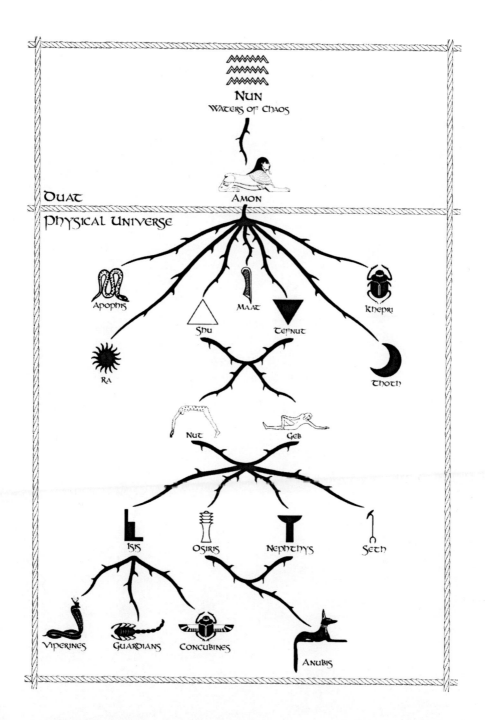

CHILDREN OF ASET
THE ASETIAN VAMPIRES

A setians are the primordial vampires. Without a human soul, they are otherkin beings that represent the immortal bloodline of the Gods. The Children of Aset trace their roots back to the Ancient Egypt, a land of magick, religion and temples...

The use of the word *Asetians* does not refer exclusively to the three primordial Children of Isis, but to the whole bloodline that derived from them. Their birth to darkness, what is sometimes called to their vampiric nature, occurred during a period that the Egyptians knew as *Sep Tepy*, which translates to *First Time*. The time of the Gods, where Isis and Osiris walked this very earth, and together with the other divine powers left the knowledge that was late to be used by the Egyptians to grow into one of the most advanced civilizations the world has ever seen.

The vampires of the House of Aset, the Order of Aset Ka, are not vampires from fiction or myth, nor are they new-age psychic vampires alike. They belong to a very specific metaphysical breed, or otherkin bloodline, born thousands of years ago. Long dead and reborn, in an ever-changing world, their souls linger forever and, in silence, they walk among us.

Calling themselves the immortal Children of the Gods, they are not really human, even though you probably would not tell a difference between one and yourself, at least if not being adept at metaphysics and energy sensing. Occult inside the societies of this world, they endure... the predators of mankind.

Vampirism

A thought that is always subject to some confusion and misinterpretation in the Asetian mysteries is the vampiric nature of the Asetians. But what exactly is a vampire?

Most of the general human knowledge about vampirism is based on the vampires from myth and lore. From the classic of fiction – *Dracula* – which took the Irish writer Bram Stoker in an eight-year research about the vampire myth and European folklore, that despite being originally published in 1897, it is still sold today; to the romanticized vampires from New Orleans in the novels of Anne Rice, where some of her main characters from the *Vampire Chronicles* share their fictional world with a very real one, like the vampires' residence on the Rue Royale, not far from the St. Louis cemetery, one of the oldest in the country.[1]

But the fact is that these stories and tales are very far from the true nature of real vampirism. The same goes for the medieval lore and whole conceptualization of vampires, where they were described as real monsters that arose from their own graves at night to seek the blood of the innocents, still far from the vampires' true origin.

"But first, on earth as vampire sent,
Thy corpse shall from its tomb be rent.
Then ghastly haunt thy native place,
And suck the blood of all thy race."
- George Byron

Vampires and similar creatures can be found in nearly every culture around the world. The tales of the Vetalas from India are found in the Sanskrit folklore, vampire-alike demons called Lilu are known from the mysteries of Babylonia, and even before, the bloodsucking Akhkharu were seen in the Sumerian mythology. In fact one of these female demons, named Lilitu, was later adopted by the Jewish demonology as Lilith, being an archetype still currently used in some ritualistic traditions of the Left Hand Path. But most of the well-known lore of the vampire comes from the Romanian and Slavic tales, the so-called Strigoi, Nosferatu and Varcolaci, among others.

However, the true vampire, as a real being and not the concept found around the word and in history as pure myth created by man, has its roots on Ancient Egypt. These dark beings have been known under many different names over the centuries, being the name *vampire* a more recent word, used to define these *creatures of the night.*

When we refer to the *vampire* concept, the most basic and intrinsic definition is any sort of being that drains life force from others. This assumption is correct, even though their motivations and reasons are often misunderstood. Thus, the essence of the vampiric nature is then never fully comprehended.

We will explain the nature of the vampire under an Asetian view, but keep in mind that this is applied to *Asetian Vampirism,* and does not define all the types and variations of the vampiric nature of all beings.

The transformation that the Asetian Elders have undergone thousands of years ago made them what they are, for the good and the bad. The great metaphysical abilities and mastery in energy manipulation are a characteristic of the nature of the Asetians, like the access to a more conscious control over the reincarnation cycle. Also because of this divine nature, the energy body, Shen Centers and soul of the Asetians are not just like their human counterparts. This difference in subtle anatomy represents the reason behind the vampire's energy need. The highly developed energy metabolism demands a higher level of energy to maintain its internal balance while incarnated and to fuel the energy abilities and powers.

A human energy system constantly draws energy, at different rates and speeds, from the universal source, to maintain its own system and aura. Some work very efficiently, but others not as good, manifesting in different problems, both subtle and physical, but almost invariably starting with energy stagnation. However, a vampiric system cannot be kept stable and sane under the regular universal energy cycling alone. While this normal energy cycle does stabilize their aura and can be used in a variety of energy manipulation techniques and healing, it does not support their own internal energy metabolism. Despite needing a higher level of energy, a vampiric system also needs it in the form of different vibrations and frequencies. This is the main reason why vampires need to rely on other sources of energy, like elemental and residual energies, but mainly on direct vital energy drains from humans, defining the reason why they are called vampires.

The vampires' need for vital force and the action of draining it from human beings is one of the most feared subjects under the majority of the population aware of the existence of their kin. This is not only due to the common myths about vampires as being fearful predators and evil beings, but also to the modern new-age currents and defensive literature, that commonly describe the vampire as something that everyone should protect against, without any attempt at trying to firstly understand its true nature.

Should we believe that all of these myths, theories and fears are wrong? No. But we can surely say that a better understanding of the vampire is crucial and probably even better than all the defense techniques that students from the new-age traditions acclaim to possess. While vampires are indeed predatory beings that can respond with damage and even lethal power if provoked, it is not entirely true that the majority of the community does attack and harm people for no well-founded reason. Most of the vampires are kept to themselves, and just don't want to be disturbed about their inner matters by people outside of their metaphysical circle. Also, while a vampiric energy drain can be harmful to the victim's energy system, on both physical and mental levels, a controlled and cautious drain from an aware donor, by a responsible vampire, can actually facilitate healing, promote new and fresh energy to be absorbed and cycled through the system and even prevent malignant stagnation. So, not all of the consequences from vampiric actions are harmful, and actual people that can consciously rely on the vampires' abilities with energy manipulation, could be considered blessed and should certainly value it and treasure it, without fearing the nature of the vampire out of misunderstanding.

Despite the positive vampiric influence described above, the irresponsible actions of a predatory being can be devastating. So caution is always recommended when contact is being established with an unknown vampire. Their metaphysical mastery can be potentially harmful when compared to the human ability to manipulate and control energy. And while the vampires' drain can have positive effects, it can also be very dangerous if uncontrolled and, in some cases, even lethal.

> *"Dare we risk ignoring a force whose*
> *strength lies in the fact that no one*
> *will believe in its existence?"*
> - Sean Manchester

Vampires from mythology – *vampyres* in archaic spelling – are said to subsist only by the ingestion of living blood from other humans or animals

– hematophagy – and share many other abilities, that even though unrealistic for the real vampire, its inclusion in the lore of the vampire can be easily understood on a metaphysical and energetic approach.

The blood connection is obvious, and even though real in its concept and substantiated through the study of subtle anatomy, it certainly cannot sustain a living vampire only by the ingestion of it. This procedure is done to sustain only the energy system of the vampire and not to feed his physical body, which can be better understood in the following section about *blood*.

Another well-known power of the vampire is his ability to fly and shape-shift. This connection is better understood under the light of astral traveling. Many vampires are adept at projecting themselves into the astral realm and through dream techniques as *dreamwalking*. While in the astral plane, a vampire easily changes his appearance, shifting from young to old and vice-versa, also adopting animal forms, where the most common are the bat, wolf, cat and snake. These forms give them special qualities in the astral realm, from the mastery of flight to strength, night vision and poison. The same goes for the flying myth, since it is possible to fly, become smoke or mist, with some mastery over the astral plane, being the true reason behind these connections with vampirism. Real vampires do not fly nor shape-shift in the physical realm, even thought they can sometimes induce someone's thoughts and eyes to imagine those traits, which is a whole different vampiric power – manipulation.

This power is related with the ability from the vampire to channel and manipulate mind energy, affecting its vibrations and frequencies, which manifests under different levels, but represents the main source for the vampire myth of invisibility. As it is possible for the vampires to read the mind of others, at some extent, they can also induce someone to look at them and clearly notice their presence, or to turn their faces away and keep walking without giving any special focus to the being present in the surroundings. This ability of the vampire to manipulate the mind and senses of humans through energy can be misinterpreted as having the power to become invisible, which is of course not true.

Another of these myths resides in the more-than-human strength of the vampire, that is completely wrong in the sense of real vampires, that in fact tend to be physically weaker than humans because of their fragile connection with the physical realm, but that can, unlike most of the humans, fuel their physical strength with energy. This is a reason that can, in particular circumstances, make a vampire look stronger, as for example in a physical confrontation, something that is most of all very rare for an Asetian to be involved in, especially with humans as targets.

Like all these examples, the myths of the vampires describe them full of fascinating abilities, where most should not be literally interpreted, but understood under a more occult and metaphysical approach.

But how did the vampire change from the horrors of myth to the sensual, and many times sexual, attractiveness of the creature seen in the modern age? The answer is simple: archetype.

Today, the vampire is many times seen not only as a fearing predatory creature, but also as the personification of our truest, most secret and obscure desires, thoughts and feelings. But unlike everyone else, the vampire does not condemn himself for all of those desires; he does not run away from them... He lives them. It is easy to picture a beautiful girl lustfully uncovering her neck or wrist to the powerful vampire awaiting her, and this is not always drawn from the power of the vampire manipulating her, but can also be the true manifestation of that girl's secret desire, that in other situation would be kept secret and the possibility to expand and manifest itself would never be fully given.

Blood

The word *blood* is a common factor in many discourses about vampirism. Unlike many supposedly vampiric traditions, Asetianism does not claim that the relation between blood and vampirism is purely mythological and has no real importance to the modern vampire. However, its relation to vampirism is nowhere near anything that is seen on the wide screen or read in fiction.

Blood is the most widespread energetically charged substance, closely followed by semen and vaginal fluids, which under the proper conditions can even surpass it in terms of energy concentration and intensity. This is something that is easily understood to anyone with basic notions of subtle anatomy. The *organs* that control and guide the energy inside the subtle body – called by the Asetians as *Shen Centers* but known out of the Kemetic culture as *Chakras* – are all connected by energy filaments, called *meridians*. The meridians work in a similar way to the physical blood vessels, and are to some extent aligned with them. Some are larger and stronger, allowing a higher stream of energy to pass through, while others are very thin and fragile, just like the veins and arteries in the physical blood system.

Because of this proximity and alignment, the blood circulating inside the human body will always have a high energy charge, being an ideal substance for vampiric feeding. Because of the volatile nature of the energy, if blood is left out of the human body for some time, energy will deteriorate and dissipate, and the blood will eventually become uncharged. This is the main reason why dead blood will never feed a needed vampire and why blood feeding is done directly from a living donor and never conserved out of him for feeding purposes.

Blood is not only a metaphor for vital energy, which is a notion that is getting more commonly spread as a misconception in the new-age vampire communities, that have come as far as making bizarre vampiric rules that strictly forbidden the use of blood. All of this is maintained by people with no knowledge on metaphysics, making those false claims and creating fictitious tenets that mostly fulfill their needs for a role-playing community and everyday getting increasingly distant from the real vampiric one. Blood has been used on both vampiric practices and witchcraft for ages, and while it certainly is a potent symbol, that is also used in some practices as a tool for the projection of Will, its function surely isn't only a metaphor for energy, but a vessel for life force itself. However, acknowledging this, many vampires don't even use blood as a feeding source, relying on more advanced metaphysical techniques to drain vital force from humans and nature. But they are still aware of the connection between blood and energy, and how highly charged the substance is with the vital force of its owner, not neglecting its use, power and applicability as a tool, not only to the unconscious mind and Will, but also to actual magick, energy manipulation and metaphysics. The same goes for other highly charged substances, like sexual fluids and saliva, which also retain living Ka, impregnated with the fingerprint and essence of their owners.

> *"I am the redness which came forth from Aset.*
> *I am the blood that issued from Nebt-Het.*
> *I am firmly bound up at the waist, and there is*
> *nothing which the Gods can do for me.*
> *For I am the representative of Ra, and I do not die."*
>
> - Pyramid Texts

In the vampiric subculture it is common to see the vampire divided into two different categories: the *psychic* and the *sanguinarian* – more correctly called *sanguinarius*, from the Latin.

While these two definitions can be established in the form of feeding types and techniques, they cannot be truly differentiated on a real vampire analysis. The psychic vampirism refers specifically to vampires that feed by draining vital energy from living beings or the environment without the need to draw blood and usually without physical contact, sometimes also called pranic vampirism. While the sanguinarians are connected with the vampires that ingest physical blood from humans to feed their energy needs. The fact is that any true vampire can feed in both ways. While some have such a peculiar energy metabolism that draining blood is almost essential to maintain its subtle balance, others can rely on energy drains only, without any physical substance involved. At the same time, any sanguinarian vampire can and does drain vital energy by psychic means. So despite the separation found in the vampire lifestyle community, there are no psychic vampires apart from sanguinarian ones — a true vampire is both. The feeding being strictly psychic or also sanguine will reflect the vampire's internal energy system, or more commonly just an option, ethics and above all, personal taste. These are also the main reasons why some vampires feel drawn towards blood, a feeling they sometimes call as an *uncontrollable thirst*, but also not reflected in every vampire. To vampires with a lower energy metabolism, they can even have no feelings at all towards blood.

"Her blood coursed through my veins sweeter than life itself."
- Anne Rice

As many things within the vampire subculture, there are no defined rules and defaults. While blood donors to sanguinarians are mostly people intimate to the vampire and are certainly aware of what is happening and giving their own blood willingly, there are cases where the blood is drawn by vampiric attacks, from unwilling donors. This will be related with the ethics and preferences of the vampire. However, particularly for the Asetians, it is more than common that they are only willing to blood-feed from another Asetian, since they give a major importance to the quality and purity of the blood and don't want to be mixing their sacred essence with, possibly polluted, human blood.

The concept of vampires, vampirism and its relation with blood is present in nearly every culture, religion and philosophy known to man, many times disguised under symbolism, and others implicit quite directly in their system. This can be even found in the religions that try the most to run away from vampires and become detached with these dark paths. In Christianity, the drinking of the blood of Christ is a concept purely metaphorical and symbolic, but nevertheless completely vampiric. The drink of the blood from the master to attain his blessing and God's blessing, opening the door to immortality and by this achieving eternal life, is all so visibly connected with the ancient Asetian concept of *Dark Kiss*, that it hardly passes unnoticed to anyone knowledgeable on vampirism. The Dark Kiss represents a blessing not only from the Asetian master, but also from the divine Aset, just like Christianity connects this symbology to a blessing from Jesus and God, the earthen master and the divine one. And to increase this parallelism, it is through the Dark Kiss that a vampire achieves immortality, conquering his own eternal life. This is not an isolated case or coincidence. Just like Christianity, many other religions and world traditions have reminiscent aspects of the ancient vampiric paths originated in the Asetianism, that can be studied and analyzed by anyone familiar with this kind of symbolism and spirituality.

Religion

Religiously, the Asetian culture is very diverse, with the basics and roots of its spirituality tied to the ancient Kemetic theology. The traditional Kemetic system can be considered the first real religion of mankind, from where most of the modern doctrines found around the world trace some roots and draw many adapted dogmas and concepts. Despite this obvious connection, the spiritual nature of the modern Asetian draws much knowledge from the comparative study of world religions.

> *"Impermanent are all created things.*
> *Strive on with awareness."*
>   - Siddhartha Gautama

Not only this religious study pursuit works as an anchor for the philosophical development of the Asetian, as it is also a valuable tool in past-life work. Since the Asetians have been born – reincarnated – in many different cultures, with different religious pillars and social structures, the study of these societies and their spiritual beliefs is an important asset, working as a subliminal access point into this sort of memories stored in the *Akashic Records*.

Asetians are not easily established or identified within one single religion found among the practices of the world. This is, among many things, due to the rigid dogmas of the worldwide major religions and their typically static tenets. Despite this analysis, Asetians tend to be beings of deep spirituality, easily connecting with nature, energy and the subtle realms, but living their own religion in a more free and personal way. Also, the vast majority of current religions are aggressive towards vampires and vampiric traditions. From the large dominant ones, like Christianity, that sees vampires as devils incarnated, to more modern movements like the Wiccan faith, from the new-age currents, which clearly states vampires as a danger and an evil that everyone should learn to defend from.

The Asetian tradition being deeply entwined with Kemeticism, is directly connected to the concept of polytheism. While the dominant Abrahamic religions, with common roots on the Semitic tradition and tracing their foundations to Abraham – like Judaism, Islam and Christianity – are typically monotheistic, there are various arguments to explain how the definition of a single god-form, or divinity, is derogatory of the divine essence itself. For the Asetians, like for the Ancient Egyptians, the divinity is something tremendously complex that manifests in many different aspects, having infinite forms, faces and possibilities. To adapt this concept, impossible to conceive to the mind when inhabiting this jailed physical world, the polytheistic view of the divine is a close approach to analyze, discuss and meditate about something that is in fact impossible to fully comprehend or to translate by words and symbols. In this way, the divine essence is represented in its many forms and under distinct behaviors, resulting in the Egyptian pantheon. The divine is not good or evil, nor strong or weak. Like nature can give you life, water and food, it can also be an abusive destroyer, with storms, quakes and tornados. This duality is present everywhere and in everything. This complex notion of divinity was ever present in the ancient Kemetic traditions, where definitions can easily be found for around 500 deities, but where the existence of known Gods and

Goddesses manifested in more than 1500 faces of the divine, giving a glimpse of that notion about infinite manifestations and forms.[2]

Another important factor in the Asetian and Kemetic religions is the existence of different faces from the same divinity. Many deities, despite their known differences and characteristics, are just different forms and manifestations from the same particular energy of the global divinity. Typical examples are Sekhmet and Bastet, both Kemetic Goddesses that can be seen as separate, but are also different manifestations of the same divine energy. Both feline deities, the cat-headed Bastet is more docile and protector, ruler of war in the Lower Egypt, while the fierce lioness Sekhmet is the dark aspect of Bastet, representing the *Scarlet Woman*, and one of the known Goddesses with a bloodlust towards mankind. In an ultimate analysis, they are both two different manifestations of Aset, the Goddess of many faces. This is called *syncretism*, and is the concept used in religion to define the connection between disparate forces that can in fact be seen as one. It was due to this highly elaborate use of syncretism found in the Kemetic religion that the concept of Isis being the Goddess of 1000 names arose, since many Goddesses explored within the Ancient Egyptian mysteries were in fact different faces, forms and manifestations of the always-changing mighty Aset.

Something hard to conceive and accept to the followers of the monotheistic religions is the main link that connects them to Kemeticism. In the time of the Egyptian Gods there was no concept of monotheism, the theology was based on the concept of multiple god-forms as explained before. In the Eighteenth dynasty, a pharaoh called Amenhotep IV reached the throne of Egypt, to be known as Akhenaten – meaning *Servant of the Aten*. This reformist pharaoh created his own religion, based on one single powerful God – the Aten. With this move, Akhenaten tried to transform the millenary Egyptian religion into the monotheistical worship of the Aten, becoming the first known religion creationist in the history of mankind. The Atenism, cult of the solar sun-disk, endured during Akhenaten's reign, against the beliefs and will of the Egyptian people and priests, still devoted to their ancient religion.

Immediately following Akhenaten's death, his reign was defaced, his beloved capital Amarna abandoned and his belief system destroyed, abolished from the Egyptian realms. The Egyptians didn't want to bear any more heresy and nonsense from an insane and egocentric pharaoh. But his beliefs endured in silence...

Later in history, Moses, a Hebrew that was born in Egypt and adopted at a young age by the Egyptian royal family, left the country together with other Hebrews, taking them through the Red Sea and into the desert. Some of these people were the remaining followers of the Atenism, the fallen religion created by Akhenaten. These teachings and beliefs led Moses to many of his writings, including the Torah, and in his own way recreating the religion of Abraham – Judaism – so it could develop to what it is known today. This movement alone would transform the world of religions forever. The Torah is part of the Tanakh, forming the Hebrew Bible, and it is composed by five books known as Genesis, Exodus, Leviticus, Numbers and Deuteronomy, which are also the first five books from the Christian Bible, referring to the Old Testament. These texts also represent a clear influence in the Qur'an, the holy book in Islam and central religious text to Muslims. In this way, together with the Abrahamic roots, it is easy to understand how Judaism eventually gave birth to the religion that followed Mohammed's teachings – Islamism – and in its own time would lead the rising of the giant known as Christianity, theoretically following the words of Jesus.

All this is the forgotten historical truth that many followers from the monotheistic religions don't like to remember when talking about their one, sovereign, God – the fact that their simple divine theory and the whole foundation of their own religion derives from dogmatic beliefs created by a hated pharaoh and the egocentric ideas of a delusional king. Nothing more than a small religion that was discontinued and abolished on the first chance, and then forever forgotten by the true Egyptian people – the followers of the Gods.

Isis as a Dark Archetype

Throughout the modern times, Isis has been seen as a beautiful, caring and loving Goddess, a symbol of light and peace. While this definition is not entirely incorrect, it is undoubtedly incomplete. This is mainly due to wrong interpretations from Egyptologists concerning the Egyptian myths and the nature of the pantheon. Many are true connoisseurs of the Egyptian language and culture, but most have no knowledge whatsoever of religion, spirituality and occultism itself. How can someone truly understand the essence of the world's most complex religious system without even being a believer?

Isis, the Greek name for the Egyptian Aset, was in fact a Goddess of many faces and manifestations, which can be referred under a view of divine duality. The truth is that Aset is caring, loving and even overprotective, but can also manifest as a darker archetype. How can the most dangerous Goddess of all time be seen only as a manifestation of light and love? She certainly shares the greatest love of all for Her children – the Asetians – but She also shows vengeance towards all that go against Her will and do not respect Her divine bloodline.

One of the many simple examples of the darker aspects of Aset is the documented history from Her conquer of the secret name of Ra. The Sun God Ra was the leader of the Gods at the time, In the Sep Tepy, a true God among the Gods, until he was poisoned by the trickery magickal powers of Aset, which got him completely at Her mercy. Isis, already a powerful Goddess, wanted that power; She would never bow to a superior God, especially a burning, arrogant one. She only released Ra from Her controlling powers when he gave Her his secret name, which symbolically represented his mighty powers among the rest of the pantheon. This episode is a clear example of the interests of Isis in achieving a higher power, and how can the sweet, beautiful Goddess, easily transform into a frightening, powerful and dark Goddess, far more evil than Her twin sister Nephthys, a funerary deity more commonly described by scholars as the darker one. And how wrong they were on that analysis and interpretation...

So, Aset can be seen as both darkness and light. She is both. Complete. And Her true nature, intentions and archetypical form should never be thought of lightly.

Vampires as Healers

Despite all that comes with the predatory nature and inborn power of the vampires, they shall not be seen only as something dangerous that should be feared. In fact, when their energy abilities, intuition and incredible spiritual insight is applied towards healing, they can achieve outstanding results, commonly many times more effective than humans using the same techniques.

This is one form to perceive the power of the duality paradigm in vampirism. Their darker aspects are also what allow for the powerful beings of light that they can be to manifest.

Despite the typical healing techniques and traditions from the ancient vampiric culture, especially the Ancient Egyptian medicine, practiced by the Asetians, they can also become great practitioners on a myriad of alternative medicine branches, and traditional medicine systems like the ones found in China and Japan, with their own specialties like Acupuncture, Acupressure and Shiatsu, or the Ayuvedra found in India. Their ancient knowledge can be applied to different types of holistic medicine, from homeopathy to herbology and crystal healing. But their greater strength is on the energy-related healing techniques and medical practices. Systems like Reiki, among many others, are easily mastered by an Asetian with basic metaphysical knowledge and practice with energy manipulation.

One of the most incredible things about vampiric healing, and commonly the most misleading because of its predatory nature, is the fact that a vampire feed can in fact heal, under the right circumstances. This exclusively vampiric ability gives them a great tool that usually is not accessible to a human therapist, being a very potent technique to break stagnated energies and even tumor centers inside the subtle body. A vampiric drain can be very dangerous and even lethal, if misused. However, when done in a controlled and responsible way by the vampire, can promote very healthy states on their donors, or patients, in the case of being a therapist or medical doctor. The small and consistent drains promote a healthy flow on the subtle body, that will echo to the physical and manifest in good health, while more intense drains can break stagnated energy that would manifest on the physical body in the form of diseases, emotional problems and unbalances.

Ankh

The Ankh, ancient symbol of Life, is the Egyptian hieroglyph that literally means *life*. The Ankh is one of the most sacred symbols for the Asetians, where they interpret it as meaning *Eternal Life*, a mark of their own immortality. This is the main reason why the symbol is found in almost all of the Asetian texts, rituals, practices and talismans. It is also common for an Asetian to wear the Ankh as a symbol of his own divine, vampiric and immortal soul, something that he wears with pride and honor, being sacred to him.

With the advent of the new-age philosophies and modern mystical traditions, the symbolism of the Ankh, already very popular among many sects, was even more popularized, becoming common the use of the symbol as adornment and jewelry in different subcultures, especially in the occult communities, even by people without any profound relation with the symbol, its culture and past. This situation is something that is generally very criticized by the followers of the Asetian tradition, which consider this vulgarization of the sacred Ankh a lack of respect, meaning, and above all, a great lack of personality. This popular spread of the symbol, where many people started wearing it just out of fashion and to give themselves a little more occultist look, is something that can be parallel to the reason why so many people are seen in the gothic-fashion community wearing crosses, with no symbolism to them whatsoever.

Dark Mark

The Dark Mark is something exclusively Asetian, even though it was adopted and copied over the centuries by different traditions, covens and groups. Much information has been debated about the concept of the Dark Mark over the time, and much speculation about it exists even nowadays. The Dark Mark is something sacred, religious and very profound, that is taken with much respect, appreciation and honor by every Asetian.

During the Sep Tepy, the Asetian Elders practiced a sacred technique within the temples that was able to metaphysically tattoo the very soul, engraving magickal symbols into the core of someone's inner essence. These sacred rituals were born from the technique that Aset passed on to Her primordial children, and based on the initiation that She had Herself done to them. During these days, the Order of Aset Ka was known by a powerful sigil, a sacred symbol created by Aset Herself, as a holy mark of Her own divine bloodline. The Primordials engraved this symbol in the wrists of their initiates – like Aset have done to them long before – and into the core of the subtle system. With secret rituals they empowered the sigil, and then Aset blessed it with Her sacred essence – the *Violet Flame*. This became the definite mark of the Children of Aset, the sacred sigil of the Aset Ka and their protected Asetians, being called by some as the Dark Mark. Working also as a metaphysical sign, so that the Elders could be drawn to each other after death, and in every single incarnation, the Dark Mark occults within itself many secrets.

The infamous Dark Mark is a renowned symbol of the vampiric lineage of the Gods, that have lingered with its same power into modern days, where it is more commonly recognized by the physically represented form – the sacred tattoo. The metaphysical mark is eternal, engraved in the Asetians' own soul forever, but the physical one is not. Since the body is not eternal and dies, so does the physical mark, needing to be recreated in every incarnation. This procedure is done after the awakening, and only by the Aset Ka, where a tattoo of the Asetian sigil is engraved in the skin of the vampire's wrist, according to ancient rituals of blessing and sacred initiation. This physical mark hooves above the metaphysical one, bounding to each other, and empowering a link with their essence and initiation in the Sep Tepy period.

Being a sigil, the Dark Mark is surrounded by symbolism. On a more direct and basic level, the sigil embraces three distinctive symbols: the Ankh hieroglyph, symbolizing the Asetian conquer of immortality and their right to eternal life; the Wings of Isis, connecting to the sacred Asetian genesis and divine bloodline of the Gods through the essence of Aset; and the Rays of Isis, usually represented on the top of the head of Aset and Her other manifestations – like Hathor – in Her Crown Shen, and also here symbolizing the sacred metaphysical connection to divinity through these two rays of energy – the Violet Flame. This is the most easily drawn symbolism from the Asetian sigil, that within itself has hidden meanings far more profound, and sustains even more complex symbolism and knowledge of the ancients, uncovered behind the veil of this lost powerful symbol drawn by Aset Herself. The whole Mark embraces ancient symbolism, secret mysteries and sacred proportions, where even the Wings that fly forth from the eternal Ankh are structured into three different layers, as a reflection of the triple nature of the Asetians, through the three Children of Aset – the Asetian lineages.

Unlike most of the symbols tattooed on the wrist, the Asetian Dark Mark is always tattooed facing the Asetian, with the lower end of the Ankh pointing to the inner arm and the Rays of Isis pointing out to the hand and into the outer world. This characteristic alone is purely vampiric and symbolic in nature as well, since the Mark is engraved in a way that is perfectly seen by the Asetian at all times, but usually seen inverted by the common world. This symbolizes the divinity inside every Asetian, where the symbol works not as an object to show off but as a distinctive mark of his True Self.

In the end, the Asetian sigil is a hallmark of the Asetianism. Its engraving on the wrist of vampires and metaphysical usage has become more than an entity of its own, but a true legend. The full secrets and mysteries that lie within will remain hidden, under the immortal gaze of a long born creature of the ancient world.

Immortality

One of the most important pillars, concepts and beliefs in the Asetian tradition is the acceptance of their own personal immortality. This is something that is not manifested out of faith, but a thing that is considered as a fact, without the chaotic influences of doubt.

This immortality is not something physical or tangible. It is the immortality of the Asetian soul. The vital force within their Ba, that never ends nor fades away. The physical body of the vampire does not live forever; it gets old, becomes weak and perishes, just like everyone else's. But their souls linger forever, and come back to this world incarnated in a brand new physical shell – another mortal body. Just like a *Phoenix* that continuously comes back to life from the ruin of his own ashes. This cycle of death and rebirth goes on and on… until the end of time. The Phoenix has its roots in the Benu bird from Ancient Egypt, which was another symbol that in the right context literally meant reincarnation, like the Khepri.

These concepts of eternal life and never-ending rebirth are hallmarks of the Asetian religion and spirituality, being represented in two of the *Sacred Pillars* – Ankh and Khepri – Eternal Life and Transformation. However, the Pillars cannot and shall not be interpreted so easily and in such a direct way. They are symbols that express not only an idea, but also a stream of metaphysical and spiritual thought behind it. The Asetian Pillars represent a very complex philosophical system whose mysteries take years, and many times even lifetimes, to fully understand and unveil.

Being immortal, the soul of the Asetians is different from the ones present in humans, not only in form but also in characteristics. The whole way it interacts with energy is different, resulting in beings with a unique connection with the subtle. The vampiric soul not only can't be destroyed or killed, as it does not suffer any aging over time, unlike the human souls. This peculiarity in the divine soul of an Asetian conditions them, while incarnated beings, to have some problems in accepting and dealing with the old age, because while the Asetian immortal soul is ancient and full of wisdom, memories and experiences, it does not decline nor wears out. The fact that the soul of an Asetian keeps young, fresh and forever new, manifests in a higher difficulty in the adaptation to the process of getting older, both physically and mentally, while bound to this material reality. Human beings can deal a lot better with this process of aging than vampires do, because for them it is only a natural process in life, connected to their own form of existence. Their souls age and degrade with time over the cycle of incarnations, just like their bodies get weaker and die in physical life, making the process of aging and loss of faculties for them a far more natural thing in the wide scheme of things.

Past Lives

Remembrance of past lives is a valuable tool for any Asetian. This happens under many different forms, from hypnotic and energy-induced regressions, simple visions during meditation, energy work and sleep, to intuitive past life development. Of course this sort of information just by itself is not very representative, it needs to be analyzed and validated by more than one single source, before it can actually be accepted.

Invariably, if the remembrance occurs in the form of a simple flash or it manifests in a true full-fledged regression, the person has accessed his own Akashic records. The Akashic records are where all the information from past lives, in-between lives and current life are stored. To access these records is not simple, but is also a matter of predisposition as well. Some people have spent many years developing their own techniques before they could actually get any results, while some had past-life visions since their early years, and others can't access at all to the information available in these subtle records.

Things lived on past incarnations affect us all, on many different levels. From a simple feeling of attraction towards one place, to more complicated fears, likes, traumas and phobias. Of course this does not mean that everything related to this should be accepted as an influence from our ancient lives. However, these influences from past lives affect even more intensely an Asetian. In them they manifest many times far more clearer than in the human kind, since the Asetians have a thinner connection to life and the physical, and a far more strengthened connection to their Akashic records, as to their own very personal divine nature.

Sometimes, particular people and situations bring forth a feeling of connection and recognition, awakening for old memories, even if only at an unconscious level. Many things in us, that describe our ways of life, particularly after awakening, tend to reflect more ancient choices and likes from other lives, often associated with interests, talents, careers, occupations and skills that we once possessed.

"Birth is not a beginning, death is not an end.
There is existence without limitation.
There is continuity without a starting point.
Existence without limitation is space.
Continuity without a starting point is time."
- Chuang Tzu

The high importance of past-life work to the modern day Asetian is something easily understood. While much information nowadays can be accessed within the Aset Ka internal texts and members or in contact with any other awakened Asetian, most of the validation of new material can only be done with regression-based techniques and intuitive induction. Also this is the most correct way of procedure when the need to confirm old theories arises. One of the most common procedures developed inside the Aset Ka Order and used in cases of validation of past-life work is what we call *Triangulation*. This technique, that involves regressive, intuitive and magickal work from three different Asetian Elders, one from each Lineage, allows a more correct and precise analysis of the material, and a greater level of error correction.

The past is what we are. We are here today just because of it. All we represent is condensed in what we have already lived. We are affected by everything we have gone through and experienced, not only in this life, but also in all of the others before it. Even though remembrance of our past lives is important for a better understanding of our path and reasons to be here, it is not essential for us to be able to take advantage of our incarnations' background, since it is always there, despite whatever we remember. We lived, so we have learned.

Elders

Elder is a term used in an Asetian context to describe those who have been transformed during the Sep Tepy period, in the *Djehuty of Aset*.

Asetian Elders are the first of their kind, some transformed by the Primordials in person. This does not make any other Asetian vampire not a true Asetian, it just does not make them an Elder. During the current incarnation, the Elders and other ancient Asetians are not transformed with a Dark Kiss from another vampire. They are already vampires at birth, and that condition reflects on everything they are and feel.

The transformation that is done on the energy body of an awakening Asetian can theoretically be done on any human, even nowadays. But it is not a common practice for an Asetian vampire to give his Dark Kiss to just about anyone. It is a sacred and divine procedure, which any vampire would be reluctant to apply in almost any circumstance.

However, an Asetian vampire transformed in the Dynastic period, for example, or in the medieval times, is not an Elder, since it was not part of the initial group from the Sep Tepy. An Elder can be distinguished by a distinctive mark on the subtle body and other specific indicators known by the Aset Ka alone. This is only possible because the vampiric transformation practiced during the Sep Tepy is slightly different from the most modern one practiced after that period.

The three first Asetians, directly transformed by Isis Herself, are still considered Elders, although the word *Primordials* is often used to describe these very specific and special divine beings. They were the only ones transformed by Aset, and the responsible for the Asetian bloodline proliferation. Mastering the vampiric initiation of the Dark Kiss, they mimicked the mystical awakening technique used by Isis, and with Her blessing they gave eternal life and energy abilities to other humans, perpetuating the Asetian bloodline forever. The *Higher Magisterium* inside the Order of Aset Ka belongs to the Primordials, a position they always return to, incarnation after incarnation, and that no one ever occupies even if they are not around, situation where the Aset Ka is leaded by other Asetians close to the Primordials, and waiting for their return. This kind of leadership should not be seen like the typical human hierarchy, but just as the natural order of things. It was never a reason for conflicts and disputes inside the Aset Ka, which has in fact survived intact for thousands of years without any of that kind of internal problems. The Order's internal loyalty and union between members has always been one of the most powerful allies of the Asetians, where questions of leadership and power were never an issue. Being something that might be quite complicated for an undeveloped human mind to understand and accept, these matters have always been an obvious feeling for any Asetian. After all, the Primordials are not simply their friends and sacred family, but their ancestors and creators, their founders, part of Aset Herself.

Disciples

Asetian Disciple is the name used to describe any vampire, human or otherkin being, that follows the Asetian path and identifies with the Asetian tradition, structure and mysteries.

However, a Disciple does not have the Asetian vampiric transformation, needed to be an eternal Asetian vampire, but it can still follow its own nature within the Asetian tradition. In fact, a great part of the Asetian Disciples were once great allies of the Asetians, and some even fought by their side in the Epic Wars, forging with them a profound and strong connection of brotherhood.

In the ancient times, the Asetians had in their own temples many disciples, who learned the secret mysteries, alchemy, healing and magick. These people were their students, but at the same time their friends, and commonly their admirers and protectors. Some of these people are incarnated in our time. Those are the ones that feel a sense of familiarity with the Asetian tradition, and an impulse to learn more, get deeper inside the Aset Ka's circles of knowledge and reestablish that link forged so long ago.

There were also the Priestesses of Isis, human girls that in the Old Egypt devoted their lives to the Goddess Isis, working in Her temples, commonly Asetian Temples or other Aset Ka sacred infrastructures, and learning the mysteries of the Kemetic religion. Over the years many of these priestesses have been drawn to the Asetians, finding some comfort in the energies from the Holy Isis that still linger today in our world in the form of Her blessed children – the Asetians. To all these people, Asetianism is the way to live their origins and to find themselves, once again, being sometimes lost over the centuries in the wheel of the incarnation cycles. These souls, from a long time dedicated to Aset, are known as Asetian Disciples, and form an important faction of the Asetian family and religion.

Not being awakened into the Asetian vampirism by the Dark Kiss means that Disciples are not Asetians, as they are not part of their immortal bloodline. Because of this, some of the Asetian Disciples entitle themselves as *Asetianists*, because they follow Asetianism and willingly embrace the tradition with their own soul. But *Asetianist* can be called to any being that follows the Asetian path and tradition, even to the Asetians. Actually, most of the high priests and priestesses of the Ancient Egypt, when not Asetians themselves, were in fact Asetianists, following the sacred path of Aset, that was the tradition of mysteries celebrated and practiced within the temples, the dark initiatory path of the wise.

Masters

Asetian Masters are vampires, usually Elders, which have accepted under their own guard and teachings a young Disciple of the Asetian tradition, which they consider worthy of learning the secrets of the Asetian mysteries and its Kemetic tradition. These Disciples have the opportunity to become, in the future, representatives of the sacred blood of Aset, by the practice of the Dark Kiss and its eternal transformation into darkness. A Master is not only responsible for the metaphysical education of the youngster, but also to help and guide them in different subjects of occult teachings, magickal arts and philosophies.

It is common, but not a condition, for the chosen of a Master to have already been a donor, and therefore knowledgeable at some extent in the Asetian ways and mysteries.

However, it is important to take into consideration that not all Masters are defined by having an apprentice under their guidance. A Master does not need to have a Disciple under his guard to be considered one, since the concept is also connected to the level of enlightenment and spiritual evolution that the Asetian soul has achieved in the overall process of incarnations and in this current life. So there are Elders that are considered Masters just because of this definition, being a status of evolution, knowledge and respect, more than a pre-defined social position within the Order's structure, and in the occultist community.

Apprentices

One of the most cherished and sacred bonds among vampires is the close relationship of Master and Apprentice. The Apprentices of the Asetians are the Disciples chosen by an Asetian Master to become under their guard and guidance. From this point they become Apprentices, and the vampire becomes their Master. Learning the secret teachings of the Asetian tradition and how to live according to the vampiric ways, the Apprentices develop themselves, working on the mastery of a variety of occult arts and studying different religions and cultures. If someday the Master agrees that the Apprentice has earned the eternal gift of the Asetian Dark Kiss, the Apprentice becomes his *dark child* – sometimes also called as *dark angel* – after the time of initiation, and that bond lingers forever. But keep in mind that actual situations of Dark Kiss in our days are extremely rare, besides being a divine procedure only to be practiced by the Asetian Elders.

It is also common for an Asetian to call the vampire who awakened him, during this incarnation or from another past one, by Master. Some special apprentices can become donors to their Master, usually his best and closer Apprentice. This relation is sacred, intimate and powerful, and they are known as the *Dark Apprentice.* This relationship is strong and very intimate, commonly misunderstood by humans and certainly deeper than what they could ever grasp. It is characterized by an unbreakable loyalty and outstanding dedication from the Dark Apprentice, and a metaphysical bond that if cherished can linger throughout eternity.

Keepers

There is an ancient kind of beings that are inevitably bound to the Asetians in many ways. These creatures, just like the Asetians, also have a soul with roots in the Ancient Egypt. Their connection with the Asetians is close and profound, being more easily comprehended by the study of the Book of Nun – the Asetian cosmogony. They are known as Keepers.

Keepers have been, in times long past, during the Asetian Empire in Kemet, disciples of Anubis – ancient God of the Underworld – the Duat –

and later the Protector of the Dead and Keeper of the Asetians. With this intense relation with Ancient Egypt, the Keepers incarnated in our days commonly manifest a great relation with the Egyptian mythology and culture, especially Anubis, but mainly follow the Asetian tradition after their awakening.

Being also known as the *Children of Anubis*, one of the main devotions of an awakened Keeper is to protect the Asetian bloodline. This was their sacred task in the times of the Sep Tepy, entrusted by the divine presence of their father Anubis, that in most of the times, it is still honored by them in our days.

Aset was the preferred divinity to Anubis. She was the one that looked after him in the old days, before he left to the ethereal plane of the Duat, teaching him all of the magick he knows. In this way, his disciples – the Keepers – are very gifted in energy manipulation and magickal abilities, usually with a powerful intuition and control. These characteristics are an important asset in their unbreakable Will to protect the Asetians over the ages and in all their incarnations. Because of this, they are usually well respected in return by the Asetian family, many times ending up close friends with them and having an honorable position among the Aset Ka structure.

A Keeper can have a vampiric nature or a more humanized one, many times being more like a symbiotic nature than a true vampire and not being truly human either, in metaphysical terms. Still, they are classified as otherkin. While their awakening can refer to the discovery of their energy and psychic abilities, the true awakening to a Keeper is when he finally understands his importance and path along the Asetian tradition.

These great sorcerers of our time represent a very fearful detail to the enemies of the Asetians. The Keepers are forever alert, and willingly giving their lives to ensure the safety of the divine Children of Aset, like their father has entrusted them in the beginning of time.

Dark Kiss

The term *Dark Kiss* is used by the Asetians to refer to the practice, technique and moment of the transformation into a vampire, which precedes the *Awakening*. The ancients called *Khenmet* to the Dark Kiss, a Kemetic word that eventually started being used as just meaning *kiss*.

The original Dark Kiss was the moment when Aset empowered Her Children with Her own Ka, during the Sep Tepy, and spiritually initiated the first three Asetian Elders. This procedure was replicated by the Elders, in the creation of the other Asetians, establishing their own vampiric bloodline. The knowledge related with such sacred transformation will not be revealed in this book, since it is one of the most well-kept secrets inside the Asetian vampirism and traditionally only known by the Elders. This secrecy was never by no means a form of hierarchy, but a way to enforce security and purity of the tradition.

The moment when the Dark Kiss is conceded is said to be orgasmic and divine, followed by a complete collapse of the internal energy system and subtle body. This new spiritual birth changes forever their energy metabolism, giving the blessing of divinity to this being that will leave his human soul behind and embrace the darkness of immortality from now on. The transformations resulting from this new *birth* to life will reflect forever in their physical body, mental stability and emotional states.

In terms of a more ceremonial kind of magick and traditional witchcraft, the Dark Kiss could be paralleled with an initiation rite. But considering the kind of initiations practiced nowadays and in the new-age traditions, there is no connection between them and the Asetian Dark Kiss, which implies a real transformation in the initiate and not just mental inductions or placebos.

In an Asetian context of vampirism, the Dark Kiss can only be given by a Master to his Apprentice and Child – vampiric and not biological. This relationship and bond is not a simple and breakable one. The connection between an Asetian and his Apprentice is one of the most powerful forms of relation, establishing deep energy links that linger forever. These intimate relationships are sometimes tormented by obsessive thoughts towards each other and a great sense of possession. This sort of feelings and relations are many times parallel with love and other intimate relationships. Also, it is common for the vampiric child to have been already a donor from the vampire Master, which after this long metaphysical relationship decided to give the Apprentice his own eternal gift. So keep in mind that vampiric Master and Child relationships are considered sacred to most of the Asetians.

> *"You will be cursed as I am and walk through*
> *the shadow of death for all eternity."*
> – James Hart

The Dark Kiss is only possible with the consent and blessing from Aset herself. It is a vital and ultimately divine practice, where the human soul dies and the Asetian soul is born. It is a powerful process of death and rebirth, where no real words can truly describe it.

Awakening

The *Awakening* is a process that occurs after the Dark Kiss, for newborn vampires, and at some point in life for already born Asetians. It is a very complicated and confuse time for the newborn, since their internal system is passing through a lot of changes and everything will be felt in a much more intense way.

> *"That morning I was not yet a vampire, and I saw my last sunrise.*
> *I remember it completely, and yet I can't recall any sunrise before it.*
> *I watched its whole magnificence for the last time,*
> *as if it were the first. And then I said farewell to sunlight,*
> *and set out to become what I became."*
> - Anne Rice

The awakening will also be felt by any Asetian, in nearly every incarnation, when he becomes aware of his condition and true nature, now understanding many factors in his current life and recent past that were not understandable before. For an Elder, the awakening usually is not near as intense as for a newborn, since his subtle alterations in the soul did already occur thousands of years ago, and the system will just be adapting to their now aware condition, that manifests mainly energetically.

The reasons and motivations that will lead an existing but unaware vampire to awaken can be very diverse, but usually one of the most common is to become in contact with other Asetians. Also, interactions with Egyptian religion, mythology and architecture can help, among many other subliminal messages and symbols known to the already awakened.

As it is known, Asetian Elders are already vampires at birth, so even though they can be yet unawakened in the current incarnation, they still have their need to feed. This can manifest by doing it unconsciously to unaware victims, usually by inborn psychic means, and in many different situations, that ranges from social interaction to more close, direct, contact and sexual intercourse. It is also common for the unawakened to create situations that will allow them to harness a higher quantity of energy, manipulating people to achieve those situations, sometimes in an unconscious way. In this way, awakening and metaphysical training can allow the vampire to make a more conscious and controlled choice from whom he feds, as when and how he does it. But developing his abilities and powers will allow the Asetian to produce far more devastating attacks and propitiate more dangerous consequences from his feeds, if so he willingly chooses.

In some rare incarnations, an Asetian might not awaken. Even though this predatory seed is present in every single life of an Asetian, there are various reasons for this to happen. From inappropriate conditions manifested and gathered in that particular life, to a conscious choice, made before incarnating, not to awaken, which is even more rare. In some situations, even if the proper conditions are not met, the awakening might occur deriving from many different situations. On those occasions, the awakening process is more traumatic than expected, and the mind can react with a self-inducted *sleep* from his true nature and Higher Self, living only half aware of his vampiric condition and not following a vampiric lifestyle. Many times this *forgetting* is moved by the society in which the vampire lives, circle of friends and family, where the most common reason is the rejection towards their nature manifested by those around them. This situation is obviously going to further harm the individual, preventing evolution of the Self and conditioning his own personal acceptance of the inner reality. For creatures like vampires, especially Asetians, this refusal of their vampiric nature is their true mortality and, ultimately, the oblivion of their souls. Something to be highly ashamed of.

The vast majority of vampires that you will come in contact with are not Asetians. Mostly, all you will find are going to be psychic vampires with a latent and unaware vampiric condition. These vampires, like the vast majority of the unawakened, don't have any notion whatsoever of what they are, what they are capable of and why they react in some ways to the environment. Most of them don't even believe in vampires at all and have no clue that there is a vast occult society out there, functional, active and pretty much alive, living in secrecy behind the veil of common society, ruling in its very own empire of shadows.

Because of this, caution is expected when approaching an unawakened potential vampire, since it is not rare to find one without notions of the existence of a subtle reality and their latent, inborn, magickal abilities. Making it wise not to expose yourself, nor your beliefs, to someone you do not fully trust or don't know for a long period of time.

One of the greatest and oldest symbols of the vampiric transformation and rebirth manifested in the awakening is the Egyptian scarab. This symbol was also represented as a hieroglyph for the ancient Egyptians, being *Kheper* the word used to read it, which meant transformation. The Egyptian scarab symbolically covers the idea of evolutional phases that a soul passes through, before reaching a more evolved stage – Enlightenment. So, the word transmits the idea of a deep transformation, the true concept of becoming.

It is in the nature of the Egyptian scarab to lay its eggs in dung and then to roll the material until it has formed a ball from it, which will then be hardened by the sun, so it can later give birth to the winged children of the scarab. The birth of life and the flight of a new being from something as simple as a ball of dung reveals to us the subtle nature of the awakening and its mysterious ways. The scarab takes an insignificant material – the dung – and symbolically transforms it into something greater – his winged children – just like the Dark Kiss of the Asetians that transforms the mortal soul of a human into the divine soul of a God. Symbolically, the scarab gives life to something inert, as an Asetian gives eternal life to something mortal as a human, being the Khepri a direct representation of the alchemical nature of Asetianism.

Kheper-i kheper kheperu kheper-kuie em kheperu
en Khepri kheper em Sep Tepy.

"When I became, the becoming became. I have become in becoming the form of Khepri, who came into being in the Sep Tepy."

The *Kheperu Mantra* holds secrets about this obscure nature of the Asetian transformation. The resonance that arises from the constant repetition of the different forms of sound found in the mantra, deriving from the word Kheper, induces a hypnotic state that clouds the conscious mind and allows the thoughts to explore other interpretations, like a metaphysical reverberation of energy vibrations, where the message can access the subconscious without actively bumping into the rationality of the consciousness. Like a weird musical tone, the mantra resonates with the inner soul of the individual, calling forth the Higher Self, with many more planes of perception than common writing and phonetic expression would allow.[3]

Beacon

The beacon is an energy impulse, of a specific vibration and frequency, which emanates from all vampires. This is a very distinctive mark, besides the energy fingerprint, that is used by vampires to recognize one another. The signal is subtle and many times works in mysterious ways. It can be sensed by apparent attraction, something far subtler than just physical, when something just draws you closer to someone and you cannot explain why. The fact is that all vampires react to a nearby beacon, if present, and many times even unconsciously.

Like everything that is energy-related, the sensitivity to properly feel the beacon and detect it as what it is, needs training and mastery, depending on the inborn personal awareness of the individual. Lack of practice in this subject might simply result in situations that can be interpreted as a driving force to meet, look and touch at a specific person, from which the beacon is being emitted. These feelings are many times intensified by the natural heightened energy of vampires, resulting in an even stronger attraction and *thirst* for feeding from this person. In the end, the energy of the beacon draws vampires closer.

Despite what is sometimes believed about the beacon, the strength of its signal is far stronger in an awakened, trained and evolved vampire. The practice with energy work and awareness of the inner nature allows for the vampire to manifest more clearly, breaking some energy blockages that in other way would work as barriers or shields for the beacon impulses. This is why the finding of an unawakened Asetian is not usually a simple task.

Among Asetians, the beacon is more easily felt and detected by the ones of the Viperine lineage. This is due to their oversensitivity towards subtle energy and their developed connection with the Asetian source – Aset – and in this way more easily recognizing their kind better than the other two lineages. This, many times breathtaking, attraction or impulse to feed from an unawakened being with an active beacon, should not be interpreted as a subtle message to interact with him, feed from him or awaken him, but as a side effect of the beacon itself. Feeding, and especially awakening, represent serious situations that should always be followed by responsibility, awareness and knowledge.

Darkness

Another subjective theme under an occultist perspective is the embrace of darkness from the initiate. The jump into the sphere of Da'ath and the confrontation with Choronzon.

Nowadays it is common to use the definitions of Left Hand Path and Right Hand Path to describe two different and somewhat opposed paths within the myriad of occult traditions available. It is also common to parallel Left Hand Path and Right Hand Path with Black and White Magick, while in fact true magick knows no color, nor is it defined by practicing good or evil. Those words are only perspectives, usually from a social or religious point of view, so the concepts of evil are in fact very subjective, and are not the guidelines that define the nature of the magick practices.

The dark path, or Left Hand, is a world of mystical traditions more empowered by introspection, personal evolution and development, usually more connected with the practices of High Magick. They are not so conditioned by religious dogma, are not static in nature, don't follow strict rules and always promote self-achievement and personal conquest, on an evolutionary point of view. So it is easily understood that a dark sorcerer, for example, does not implicitly practice evil magick, although he can if he so wishes. It is up to the sorcerer alone the use he gives to his own knowledge and powers, and that does not define his actions as black or white. That is defined by the techniques and knowledge he uses, as the traditions he follows, and not by the consequences of his mystical practices.

> *"On the altar of the Devil, up is down.*
> *Pleasure is pain, darkness is light.*
> *Slavery is freedom, and madness is sanity."*
> - Anton LaVey

The Asetians are by themselves creatures of darkness. This is easily seen on many manifestations, from their introspective natures, meditative workings, antisocial behaviors, elitist ideologies, magickal practices and, above all, their predatory instincts.

Vampires easily find different ways to harness their powers and fuel their abilities within the dark energies. This is related not only with metaphysical darkness but also with the physical one, since it is common for vampires to access some of their powers more easily at night and usually have a heightened sensitivity towards the Sun and bright light, many even being weakened during direct sunlight.

Chaos

The vampire himself is a representative of chaos. His own existence promotes change, attracts new energies and repels old ones, brakes stagnation and many people in contact with Asetians are almost invariably changed by them, even if it is just on something subtle.

Chaos takes us to one characteristic of an important Asetian sacred pillar – Khepri – the *Kheperu*, being the ancient Egyptian word for *Transformation*. The chaotic forces are one of the most important fuels so that Kheperu can manifest. Chaos is by itself something indefinable, something that transforms stagnation and gives it motion; it is the engine itself for change and evolution. The absence of chaotic energies implies a stagnation of the individual. Nothing compels him to adapt and evolve. He is not tested against adversities and his own personal limits, so there is no inner change, that we call Kheperu.

On a Kemetic perspective Chaos is Nothing, is the primordial waters of the abyss, where the first divine emanations appeared. Also in the Egyptian mysteries, the chaos can be parallel with the daemon-serpent Apophis, but in this manifestation being only a reflex of the chaos itself. Apophis, also called Apep, was cyclical. His daily attacks on the bark of Ra showed some coherence and strategy, which is not very chaotic in nature. The same can be also understood under a *Sethian* view, since Seth himself is also a reflex of chaos. But he can also be defined in some way, having his own thoughts and patterns. He is not random; he has identity. While the pure chaos cannot be truly defined, has no rules or concepts. Chaos is Nun, the primordial ocean of nothing, where the first thoughts emerged, where life was born... the Old Gods.

Now that we have seen that Kheperu is one consequence of chaos, we can also understand that chaos itself is a tool to the vampire, an instrument that he uses and sets free so that transformation and development can occur. Vampires are the catalysts of spiritual evolution. They transform, adapt and evolve.

Heka

Heka is the Egyptian word for *Magick*, making reference to the power of words, both written and spelled. Even though the techniques used in the practice of magick are out of the subjects analyzed within this book, a reference to it was demanded, since it represents such an important and vital part of the Asetian tradition. The Asetians use magick not only to achieve their objectives, producing change with their conscious and determined act of pure Will, but they primarily rely on it as a powerful tool to aid development and evolution of the Self.

Knowing how to say the right word, do the proper gesture and induce the ideal thought, in the correct second and at the perfect cosmic moment, is practicing true magick. In that way, usually without being aware of it, many of us are magicians. However, sacred wisdom consists in knowing how to consciously do it.

> *"Heka was made for them,*
> *To use as a weapon for warding off occurrences.*
> *And so they created dreams for the night,*
> *To see the things of the day."*
> — Ancient Egyptian Papyrus

Magick is not only used in the Asetian tradition as a ritualistic reflex of old practices and ceremonial gatherings, nor does it simply rely on traditional sorcery. Asetian magick is a mix of different occult cultures, techniques and knowledge, which developed across the millennia, built on top of the ancient traditional Egyptian High Magick. The Asetian practices are far from the popular concepts of witchcraft and have been kept throughout the years as elitist practices, only available to some select few. These were usually closed communities dedicated to the study of occult mysteries and lost cultures, being historically more accessible to the ones involved in a scholar and knowledgeable sect of the occultist society. In this way, the Asetian knowledge has always been far from reach for the more traditional practices of popular occultism, whose knowledge has always been more accessible to the general public and to the ones interested in the subject. This is the main reason why this tradition has never been vulgarized like the majority of the other once more restricted traditions.

> *"The blood of Aset,*
> *the spells of Aset,*
> *the magical powers of Aset,*
> *shall make this great one strong,*
> *and shall be an amulet of protection*
> *that would do to him the things which he abominates."*
> — Egyptian Book of the Dead

One of the common translations for Heka is *The Magick of Words*. In the time of the Asetian Empire, the Asetians used the Kemetic as their main language, which was used not only among the people, as within nobility throughout the whole Egypt.

However, a sacred language known as *Serkem* was kept hidden within the temples. This language was not used for conversation or in social events, but rather in the arts of magick. It was based on the intuitive use of mantras and manifested by words of power that resulted in the real Magick of Words, the ancient Heka.

Serkem is still used nowadays in some practices, particularly by the Viperine lineage, that still empower their magical arts by this long forgotten tongue of their ancient Empire. Misunderstood among the common people, the Serkem language was usually feared by many in those days, being commonly referred as *The Black Speech* by most of the non-magickal population. This expression for the Serkem language also has its roots in the name of the Asetian Empire itself, which they called Kemet, meaning black land, so the sacred language of their temples was also a black tongue to their eyes, being both cryptic and magickal. In fact, the name of the language is a blend between other two distinctive Kemetic words – *Serket* and *Kem*, meaning scorpion and black, respectively. The first part of the language name – Serk from Serket although being the word that literally meant scorpion in Kemetic, was also a name of an important entity in the Asetian theology, the representation of the Seven Scorpions of Isis. Connecting the genesis and usage of this language not only to Aset and Her divine inspiration upon the dynamically created sacred words, but also to Her fearless daemons, which used the Serkem as their native language, an added reason to the fear of the people towards the expression of this obscure magickal language. Being the Kem part of the word also one of the possible reasons why the people knew it as The Black Speech, unlike their native language – the Kemetic – that meant *from the Black Land*.

Dark Flame

Being a purely Asetian concept, the Dark Flame is a condition that can be both invoked or manifested by the vampire, conscious or unconsciously.

It is an amorphous type of energy that manifests in the layers of the aura as a reaction to different kinds of situations. The Dark Flame manifests by heightened states of consciousness, altered mood, courage and ecstasy, many times boosting the ego. It can be triggered by common things like a social confrontation, a sense of injustice, or it can be invoked in a more ritualistic or direct manner in situations of danger and extreme conditions. The Dark Flame only manifests for short periods of time, being fueled by high streams of energy, quickly exhausting the whole energy system if done without control.

Several tools as music, ambient incense, special clothing, ritual and blood, can be used to help achieve the state where the Dark Flame manifests. These things do not influence the Dark Flame itself, but help the mind in tweaking to the altered state needed to empower it. Feelings can also be used to access this *flame*, especially aggressive ones like rage and hate, that more easily fuel it.

Despite this general analysis of the Dark Flame, its power can also be used in different ways from the ones described above and to a more positive end. It is not only feelings of rage that can fuel the Dark Flame; it is easy to make the parallel that if hate can trigger it, so can love. And in this way some vampires are able to center on that deep feelings to achieve great things and have incredible attitudes, empowering themselves with the strength of the Dark Flame, and being able to face difficult situations. In this way, many vampires can have attitudes that are easily condemned in the eyes of mere mortals, but that are driven from pure love... being highly prized among them.

In some cases, the energetic urge of the Dark Flame results in devastating behaviors and feelings from the vampire, leaving him in an agonizing mix-up of energies, completely exhausted and consumed by the intensity of this *flame*. This situation might result in the vampire getting a feeling of a sense of powerlessness towards the situation that set forth the manifestation of the Dark Flame. In worse cases, can lead to mild depression and panic. But if able to work out a solution or defensive mechanism towards the situation that caused it, it can leave the vampire in a powerful condition, with a new revamped Dark Flame, reborn from the ashes of his inner mind, like a Phoenix after its burnout.

Violet Flame

While energetically more intense as the Dark Flame, the Violet Flame has a very different nature, making it look apparently not as intense or powerful. However, the Violet Flame is actually the purest form of the Dark Flame. Hard to explain in words but easy to understand by feelings, the Violet Flame is a manifestation of the divine inside every Asetian. It manifests both mentally and emotionally, by overwhelming feelings like happiness, fulfillment and oneness.

This *flame* can be activated by ethereal touch. In simple words, metaphysical practices like effective meditation, energy work and ritual, to more mundane practices that directly affect our nature, like a one true hobby and even simpler things like listening to music and dancing can trigger it. As long as there is a divine influence, the flame is activated, sometimes referred to as the *Touch of Aset*, affecting the subtle system of the Asetian and manifesting through feelings and sensations, sometimes very intense, but other times more subtle and calming.

Unlike the Dark Flame, the Violet induces bright states of happiness and well being, working through a dump of raw energy from the seventh Shen, flooding the entire subtle system and cleansing it. Results in an expansion of the aura's dimension and brightness, and an intense projection of violet Ka, reflecting the nature and vibration of the current energetic state. Also differing from the Dark Flame, the Violet is an always-present kind of energy. When it is not activated to its full burning capacity, it lingers in the layers of the aura as a velvet and smoky energy, in the form of a soft, violet mist.

This is just a brief and ambiguous description of the Violet Flame, because its true power and interpretation is intimately related with the inner Asetian mysteries, and represents an important part of the initiatory path of the adept. Through the Violet Flame the Asetian gets more close and intimate with his source and holy genesis – Aset – being an energy manifestation that can be seen as a true religious experience. In this way it can be unveiled that the Violet Flame truly is the Essence of Aset.

> *"You live according to your Will.*
> *You are Wadjet, the Lady of the Flame.*
> *Evil will fall on those who set up against you."*
> - Egyptian Book of the Dead

Wands and Talismans

As magickal beings on their own right, it is common for the Asetians the use of magickal wands and sacred talismans. Both have a pure metaphysical use and can be used actively. This means that they work as metaphysical tools for direct energy manipulation, and are not mere ritualistic tools for the focus of Will like the ones generally used in traditional witchcraft and ritual magick.

Talismans in the Asetian tradition, known as *Wedja* in Kemetic, which also means prosperity and protection, can have different usages and can be wielded in different ways. Generally they are considered sacred instruments, bounded to their master and bearer. They can be made out of many different natural materials, being most common the use of minerals that naturally amplify energy. They are cleansed and then attuned according to the ancient knowledge of the Elders and can have many different powers and abilities, meaning that the identity of a talisman can vary greatly.

Most powerful talismans or amulets can have a servitor bounded to it, having an identity and Will of their own, and sometimes bearing a great deal of power. However, those are very rare in our days, and can only be crafted by the Elders. Also, a talisman, although commonly an object, does not necessarily need to be one. Being able to rely in the profound nature and power of symbolism, a talisman can ultimately be any object, symbol, image or even sound that can be imbued with special significance and hidden meanings behind its veil.

The whole Ancient Egyptian culture and life was surrounded by the use of talismans, in a society that understood, better than any other, the powers and usage of talismanic technology, which they learned to master. The mysterious hieroglyphs that still confuse modern scholars and amaze the world with its beauty and mystery were, in fact, a direct reflex of the talismanic technology of the ancients, reflecting a higher understanding behind the power of symbolism and talismans.[1] The Kemetic hieroglyphs that infused so many temples, papyrus and other magickal objects with power, were symbols, or sigils, that echoed secret meanings. A knowledge that could only be fully unveiled by the initiates within the ancient mysteries. They were associated with a specific thought, idea and context, but their true meanings were far broader and secret, a perfect reflex of what a talisman can accomplish in the form of a symbol. Talismanic knowledge is a typically Asetian technology, practiced and mastered from the very beginnings of their culture and empire, and used on their own sacred magick until today.

Magickal wands are also of common use among Asetians, not only as powerful metaphysical weapons, but also as very efficient energy manipulation tools and spiritual devices.

They can be made out of wood or mineral, although the more common is the use of wood because of its steady amplification of energy. Minerals are used for shorter, intense and precise wands, and sometimes they are shaped according to the mineral's own crystallography system and obeying some rules of sacred geometry, which is not always easy to craft from one single megacrystal, making the use of minerals more common in the crafting of sacred talismans and amulets.

Just like a talisman, a wand needs to be cleansed and attuned to work properly, a task that can only be done by a qualified Asetian Master, commonly called an *Encantatum*, from their expertise in energy manipulation and attunement. The wand can then be used efficiently to manipulate and direct energy, in many kinds of metaphysical work, as well as a powerful magickal weapon which, if properly mastered, can even deliver lethal attacks or conjure subtle shields of a high magnitude. Commonly, in witchcraft and other forms of magick, the wand is used as a tool in ritual for the focus of Will, which is not the case of an Asetian wand. This kind of direct usage of wands, which is used by both wizards and vampires from the secret occult society, is a tradition that goes back to the Asetians' ancient times and the crafting of the great wands of power. In time, the knowledge spread, and so did its usage. However, the Asetian wands are still seen with a great value and as a mostly desired object of power and passion. Each Asetian wand has a name and identity of its own, and many times it can only be wielded by its master. In the old days the Asetian wands became such a legend among the magickal societies that even mighty empires and kingdoms started treating their most valuable warriors' swords like the Asetians did to their wands, giving them names and treating them like almost a living extension of the warrior itself. The crafting of an Asetian wand is a sacred procedure that goes back to the secret knowledge of the Elders and that only a *Wandmaster* from the Aset Ka would know how to master. It goes far beyond the shaping of the wood into a form revealed by Aset Herself, but it is a deep, profound and mystical procedure that relies on highly complex metaphysical techniques from an Elder with a great mastery of energy manipulation and attunement. Asetian wands are precious, invaluable tools of prestige for a vampire or wizard, which retain their power for ages and are seen as authentic sacred instruments that no money can buy.

Personality

Like what has been said, explained, debated and criticized about the Asetians, they are not friendly by nature. However, this does not mean that they are easily classified as evil in every situation. That is because they are very aware creatures, innate manipulators, which even unconsciously are used to have the control of the situation and the power over the impressions that others have about them. So, they can easily be thought as friendly, if they for any reason want it to look that way.

An important fact that people usually do not know about the vampiric persona is that they really do not care if others believe in their existence, powers and abilities. Actually many of them would even prefer the general public not to believe in vampires. Their secrecy is one of their better trumps.

It can be easily perceived that it is not possible to define a whole accurate line of personality for the Asetian vampires. Like everyone else, they are very diverse, but some hallmarks are easily found within their own culture. An Asetian is usually very proud of his nature, determined about his true wishes and wills, many times eccentric, usually very knowledgeable and many times intolerant.

Many of these characteristics and traces of personality vary according to the Asetian lineage, but that will have a more in-depth look on the chapter about the different kinds of Asetians.

"We were a silent, hidden thought in the folds of oblivion,
and we have become a voice that causes the heavens to tremble."
- Khalil Gibran

Your voice alone can make a lot of noise. But your voice inside a crowd cannot be heard at all. An Asetian never tries to talk louder than the crowd surrounding him. An Asetian becomes that crowd.

Physical Appearance

Asetian vampires do not have long pointy fangs, unnatural colored eyes, long razor nails and completely white skin. That belongs to the vampires in fiction and gothic lifestyle subculture.

A subjective theme inside the vampiric influences and transformations of the Asetians is how much the physical looks and body reflects the vampire's personal energy system. While the health and physical body of the vampire is undoubtedly affected by the internal energy system and interactions with the subtle realm, easy connections and extrapolations about physical defaults and traits simply cannot be done. It is easy to observe that many Asetians tend to be pale and have some more noticeable and visible veins, at the top of their skin surface, than humans do. Especially when on low energy levels or actively interacting with it. But this cannot be taken as a rule of thumb, since there are also Asetians that do not match these specifications at all, even among Elders. However, there is truth in the myth that portrays the female Asetians with very long hair, but that is still personal choice and taste from the vampire, not a requisite or unshakable characteristic.

Despite that, there are also some attributes common to Asetians while incarnated in the physical realm. One true physical trademark among the bloodline is the characteristic circular aura around the iris of their vampiric eyes. Even though also found in humans, in Asetians this circle tends to be denser, sometimes thicker and of darker color, typically grayish. This is one of the few visible and physical marks of the Asetians.

Another characteristic of the Asetian eyes, and far easier to detect, is the depth of their sight. An Asetian vampire easily *touches* others with their gaze, transmitting behind its intense look feelings of deep knowledge, aggressive power, unrevealed secrets, and other; causing sensations on their targets that range from fear to magnetic attraction. But of course this can also be used in a manipulative way, transmitting wrong ideas of fear and frailty from the vampire.

Despite this vampiric trait from the Asetians, on a more physical level, their eyes tend to be hypersensitive, not only to bright lights – especially with ultraviolet radiation – but also to pollution in the air. In cases of exposure to sunlight or high levels of pollution, the energetic abilities of the vampire will be affected and diminished. Their subtle systems can become unbalanced and even collapse, in the more extreme cases. Actually, this Asetian sensitivity towards sunlight gives clues about the origins easily found in myth and fiction about vampires hating sunlight. Certainly any real vampire will never turn into ashes by exposure to the Sun, but it can affect him in a negative way, especially when making eye contact with the vibrations and energy of the sunrays. That mythological concept of the problems that vampires have with the Sun has two main reasons behind its genesis – one is theological and the other is metaphysical. The spiritual one is connected with the Kemetic theology, where Ra is the Sun and Thoth is the Moon. In myth, Aset commonly did not have a very good relation with the Sun God Ra, especially after the confrontation where She overpowered him, but in the other hand She was always a close friend to Thoth. This gives the first clue into the legend of a bad relation between vampires and the Sun and their connection to the Moon. The second clue is purely metaphysical, since the subtle system of the Asetians in some circumstances is not very compatible with the energy frequency of the solar radiation. So this energy, when in direct contact with their inner systems, can unbalance and weaken them, being the other reason behind why vampires do not fully master their abilities in plain day under the direct force of the Sun. However, this should not be misinterpreted. Vampires are not against the Sun, they just cannot fully embrace their higher powers while under its intense energies, or may be weakened by its presence, especially when outside of sacred ground – Kemet. But the Sun itself is of vital importance for the Asetians, who find in its times of sunrise and sunset two of the sacred moments in the Asetian religion.

Asetians have no point or interest in behaving as sexually attractive symbols. Actually, they tend to make a stand, in not being related with what is considered fashion and mainstream beauty. Despite being included in the likes of some and dislikes of others, they certainly possess a unique *feel* about their looks. An exquisite appearance that can without doubt allure to the tastes of other vampires, despite of what common mortals might feel about them.

Vampires are known to be associated with black clothes, dark and gothic themes. This is not only derived from a personal taste, but it is also used as an energy feature. Black is not a color; it is the absence of color. This means that it absorbs all the colors in the visible spectrum, reflecting nothing out of it, unlike the white, which reflects all of the colors so it is the sum of all. In this way, it is easy to perceive why Asetians use dark clothes with an energy-wise sense behind it. Being vampires, the black clothes absorb most of the energies present and circulating in the surroundings, giving their owners a better sense of the energy emanating from the people around them and the kind of subtle environment they are entering. On the other hand, wearing white clothes works as a shield, reflecting most of the surrounding energies present in the environment, leaving the individual using them much more unaware of its surroundings and possible dangers awaiting him. This is a metaphysical aspect of why the Asetians are usually seen dressing in black, and a reason that many people who just wear dark clothes out of fashion cannot truly understand and embrace. Like many other things that can be seen in an Asetian, it is not just there because of something obvious. It usually has a more deep and relevant reason behind.

Ultimately, depending on the mind, intuition and cunning of the observer, many Asetians can have a frail look about them, sometimes even vulnerable and helpless. This is typical from the vampire species, being why they have long been called wolves in the skin of a lamb. That terrifying physical presence of the vampire found on film, that makes everyone run away in horror just because of its looks, is simply fiction. The powers and dangers of the real vampires are far subtler and harder to detect than what the common and distracted mind can tell.

Otherkin

The Asetians acknowledge the existence of various other beings, both in the subtle and physical realms, that like them do not possess a human nature. All these creatures are called *otherkin*, because they do not have a human soul.

They are very diverse, each with their own characteristics and following different traditions, under a myriad of beliefs. They are also magickal entities, and most of them can manifest throughout both realities. The otherkin are out there, many times living in peace alongside humans, other times acting far more dangerously, ranging from other vampiric beings, to Anubian keepers, Sethians, Lycanthropic beasts, Draconian creatures, disembodied spirits, shades and daemons, among many others.

Like what was explained about vampires, all of these creatures also have correspondents easily found in myth and lore, which in many cases have also drawn characteristics from the real beings from which their mythological versions were created. For example, the Lycanthropic beings, commonly known as werewolves, don't have many magickal abilities, but have a highly strengthened link to the physical, giving them a lot of muscular strength, as well as endurance. Also being able to better adapt to extreme situations and weather conditions, they are shape shifters, always adopting in the astral the form of a big wolf or other similar beast. All these are directives to the common assumption that a werewolf can truly transform into a living wolf, which is not accurate. They are beings that are usually aggressive, with a tendency to be wild and rude, without a very effective self-control, especially under the influence of the energies in the Full Moon. Draconians are the reason why the myth of giant creatures with reptile look ever came to life. They are known as dragons. These beings have very large subtle bodies, a lot bigger than humans and most of the otherkin, and have an inborn ability to master the elemental of fire, using most of their magick through that hot, burning link. While they are fully human-like on the physical realm, they manifest in the astral under the form of a mighty dragon, their soul unleashed.

Vampires, as being one of the otherkin species, are not always embodied beings, meaning that not all vampires possess a physical body. There are spirits and daemons that *walk* between these worlds, fueled by the vital energy from other creatures, like the Incubus and Succubus daemons, that drive their energies from offensive sexual drains.

LINEAGES
THE ASETIAN BLOODLINES

S ince the beginning, the Asetian history has always been triple. Not only because the primordial Elders created from the essence of Aset were three, but also considering they developed in three distinct ways; each with their own specific qualities, unbalances and characteristics, especially in an energetic way.

To these different bloodlines inside the Asetian vampiric species, a different nomenclature was used, not only to differentiate between the three different sects, but also to define the mutual archetype inside each bloodline. And so we shall refer to them as *Lineages*.

A lineage is a pure Asetian concept, even though some might find similarities between religious sects, occult order structure systems, political hierarchies or social stratification castes. While this is true, parallels and correlations are not to be drawn since it is a personal Asetian-only concept, applicable exclusively to Asetians.[5]

Being Asetian specific, the true divine nature inside the vampire lineages is not supposed to be fully understood by a non-Asetian mind, and is something that is slowly unveiled by the long evolution of the soul and during each awakening, on every incarnation.

There are three, and only three, Asetian lineages: *Serpent, the Lineage of Viperines*; *Scorpion, the Lineage of Guardians* and *Scarab, the Lineage of Concubines*.

These names have changed many times over the millennia, and been known under different nomenclatures, some modern, others far ancient. Each lineage has its very own characteristics, which are most of all related with their particular subtle metabolism, energy and the way they interact with it. The differences in the specific energy system of each lineage are a consequence of the three different ways in which the subtle body can react to the Asetian vampiric transformation, but most of all it is an eternal echo of the inborn predisposition from the first three Elders – the Primordials – to be created and manifested in this world, each one the founder of each lineage, but all the three created by Aset in the first place and forever bound to Her.

The newborn soul, being divine and ultimately different from the human soul before the Dark Kiss, makes the Asetian system to manifest differently on the way he perceives, manipulates and interacts with energy, but also affects his personality, personal strengths and weaknesses, abilities and powers, and sometimes even some basic physical characteristics. In a way, redefining everything he is, forever...

Lineages, these three paths of the Asetian vampirism, are a hallmark of their whole structure. Not only functioning as a working magickal framework, but also manifesting through a whole archetypical system and a full-featured energy circle, optimized by each lineages' own specifications. Energetically, they complement each other, having the abilities of one covering the weaknesses of the other, resulting in a highly powerful closed circuit. In this triple way, energy is balanced at its peak, without stagnation and dissipation, promoting dynamism and balance of the three. Like this, they can elevate the frequencies of their own vampiric energy, making it denser, with a higher quality and vibration. However, even though of high importance, energy-wise, the metaphysical relation between the three lineages has suffered over the years. Since the long gone harmonious relation between the primordial Elders in the Sep Tepy, members of each lineage have gone through a myriad of situations over the eras, from passionate lovers to fiercest enemies. They have incarnated and met under all sort of conditions and in many different cultures. But their eternal links resist still. They are unbreakable. And even nowadays they eventually defend each other and fight for the other Asetians if the situation arises. Because the subtle Asetian links linger forever...

The following definitions and concepts, about the three Asetian lineages, are just a framework in an attempt to categorize the bloodlines. It is by no means final, static or decisive. The vampires from a specific lineage are not expected to have all the conditions described below, and they sure have different characteristics that are not mentioned in these texts. There are more specifications, currently known, to each of the bloodlines, which were kept out of this work. This was done consciously and with a specific purpose in mind. But it is important to understand that these characteristics are based on an analysis of some Asetian individuals from each lineage and according to hallmarks manifested by each of the Primordials. This does not mean that there cannot be an Asetian from one of these lineages who does not possess those characteristics or simply does not fit in the model because, as stated, it is just a very simple approach to the Asetian framework, which is not supposed to be firmly defined by words.

SERPENT
THE LINEAGE OF VIPERINES

Viperines
The Lineage of Viperines is known as the Serpent, representing
the most predatory of all immortal bloodlines, a symbol of advanced
metaphysical senses, capable of delivering unsuspected lethal attacks, being
the perfect archetype of eternal rebirth and transformation.
Viperines are undoubtedly the most rare of the Asetian kind. The first soul
to be created by Aset and lately to receive Her sacred Kiss. This lineage,
sometimes known as the *Bloodline of Horus*, is the primordial essence of the
Asetian tradition.

Despite being the first-born, they were also the ones that received a
greater impulse of Ka in the Aset's eternal Kiss, resulting in the most severe
vampiric alteration of the three lineages. While in a way this gave them
great skills to manipulate energy, powerful intuition and other abilities, it
also resulted in the most fragile physical body of the three lineages. This is
mainly because of their weakened link between spirit and flesh, that more
than just a consequence of the Serpent transformation, is a characteristic of
the Primordial Viperine – Horus.

The Asetians from this lineage are usually highly evolved beings and
prophets, with unique abilities to command and lead, who see far beyond the
horizon. These characteristics of the Viperine, being more than an ability,
but a taste, are easily recognized among their kind. While this is a powerful
attribute that can be harnessed for the good of the Asetian species, and
knowing that most of the tradition's evolution would never be possible

without Viperines' great insight and intuition, it is also a dangerous characteristic. It can become unstable and achieve huge proportions, easily transforming into the typically developed intolerance from this lineage, and sometimes heightened arrogance. This also manifests in a firm personality, many times egocentric, from whom most of all likes the sensation of victory and achievement, feeding from these occurrences many times.

Being the most physically fragile of the three, which is not always directly perceived, Viperines do not have a great connection with the physical realm, particularly their own bodies, having constant problems in grounding, and without fully *living* in our material world and society. It is typical for them to live inside their own inner world, many times not aware of other more earthly questions and issues. This is also evidenced by a highly capable creativity and imagination, which can also be harnessed, but that can turn into madness if left without conscious control.

The frailty in the physical link of an Asetian Serpent always echoes to the physical realm, manifesting through health problems. Different kinds of allergies, throat and respiratory conditions, vision and cardiac complications are the most common physical problems found on Viperines. As a result of their highly developed energy metabolism and divine soul, their subtle system never perfectly adapts to the condition of being incarnated in a physical body, commonly reflecting into this realm by a typically weak immune system and not always notorious inner anxiety and distress. Their thin bodies and pale skin are a hallmark of their physical appearance, being known attributes of the vampires easily found in myth that, just like Serpents, rarely present a developed muscular mass, without easily gaining weight. Also, their weak connection with their own bodies can be commonly perceived by lower body temperature, more noticeable on the coldness of their hands. Being owners of deep gazing, many times dark, eyes, and traditionally weak hair, because of the high flow of energy constantly flooding their Crown Shen with the profound intensity of the Violet Flame, literally burning their subtle outlets on that location, which also echoes to the physical scalp. They have a heightened sensitivity and highly active nervous system, being noticeable, for example, in the trembling of their hands. In energy crisis, their system can reach the point of collapse or, if left without conscious control and restraint, it can lead to explosive and aggressive behaviors. Most of these conditions, even though impossible to correct or cure, being a reflex of their divine soul while incarnated, can be balanced by meditative practices and energy techniques. However, the most obvious and efficient solution for balancing this kind of high demandable energy system is vampiric feeding.

Above all, the Serpent lineage has a great energy need, resulting from the highest energetic metabolism, which implies a strong need to feed directly from vital energy. Viperines need to feed regularly in order to be kept sane and stable. This can be done in different ways and under different levels, from simple direct drains done socially, to more intimate sexual drains done privately. Because of this high energy need, they do not take any relevant advantage with ambient feeding, since the energy is not only scarcer but also a lot poorer, except in some special circumstances of empowered environments. They have a very efficient system towards direct contact feeding and sexual feeding, specifically adapted to their high levels of need, but they can also effectively feed from the environment when in sacred ground – their native lands in Egypt.

Spiritually, they tend to be the counselors and guides of the Asetian family, being the ones that more easily connect with the Asetian energies and mysteries, having a great insight into the philosophies and concepts of vampirism. They possess the higher charge of the Violet Flame over their essence, which is a great asset in the connection to the Asetian source – Isis – and the development of that intimate bond.

While their internal system is not the most chaotic of the three, they are the ones that more easily induce change over the environment and with everyone they interact with. They easily shift minds, ideas and even established dogmas of others. While this can be very useful for a responsible Viperine, it also can be dangerous if exploited for his own personal interests without regards of ethics and respect.

Being the ones that promote a more dramatic change in others, it is normal to see friends, and even more commonly lovers, to adapt to that very peculiar nature of the Serpent, with their own likes and dislikes, and in this way forging a stronger link to better completing each other and deepening their bonds. However, this transition and adaptation is not always pacific and subtle. If the nature of the other one is very static and stagnated, that can result in damage to his psyche and mental stability. Which in worse cases can lead to psychological problems, or even to the jailing of the other one's mind into the life, world and creations of the Viperine.

Unlike Guardians and more close to the psyche of the Concubines, Viperines are commonly more dependant creatures. But that manifests on a very different level than the one found in Concubines, since Viperines hardly connect with humans and traditionally are not very social. Their true bonds are clearly more directed to the Asetian family and their deep intimate links. Even though they might not let that trespass to others, their frailties, sensitivities and powerful energy signatures demand the support and presence of others. Loneliness can easily unbalance their energy system and echo into the mental realm, commonly manifesting through depression, sadness, bad moods and sometimes even aggressive behaviors. However, and like previously stated, this does not manifest towards everyone, but just with the more close and intimate relations of the Viperine, that are the only ones for which they truly care about.

According to the principals of duality, of major importance within the Asetian tradition, the Viperines have the most balanced energy body when referring to sexual polarity. They can see through both points of view and perspectives, with the power to analyze things under masculine and feminine mindsets, having the energies of one and the other, naturally mingling both polarities under the same host, despite what body they might incarnate.

Viperines are usually the most *desired* among the three lineages, since they are the ones who gather inside them greater mysteries. They are the ones that more easily project their aura, adapting it to the receivers' tastes and likes, being highly adept at all sorts of manipulation – energetically, mentally and socially. Asetian Serpents are true natural pretenders, easily *transforming* into something they want just to impress their targets, gaining their trust and admiration, becoming remarkably easy for them to pass by different types of people virtually undetectable. This is an ability that while being a potent trump, can leave the Asetian in mental instability if not used with caution and control. So while they are extremely trustworthy beings for their closer friends and lovers, they are very dangerous for the outsiders. When this is added to their inborn agility towards energy and magick, makes the Viperines clearly the most feared among Asetians.

SCORPION
THE LINEAGE OF GUARDIANS

G

uardians

The Lineage of Guardians is known as the Scorpion, representing their antisocial behavior, advanced defensive mechanisms, highly protective nature and strong personality. The scorpions found in the wild, very common in Egypt, are known for being aggressive when touched, just like Guardians. In the ancient times it was believed that they would sting themselves with their own venom when trapped in a deadly situation, reminding the choice made by some of the ancient vampiric donors and wives to kill themselves if their honor was tainted or if their masters were dead. A situation known in the Asetian culture as the *Deadly Poison*. Despite its symbolic nature, Guardians also earned the parallel with the Scorpion since some of the Elders were known to incorporate the elite army of the Imperial Guard. Although not the only ones, these special Guardians, powerful masters of metaphysics and strong experts in warfare, were personally trained by the mighty Scorpion daemons of Aset, being also one of the reasons why they were connected with this powerful symbol in the Asetian culture and Kemetic life. But Guardians should not be mistaken as the Scorpions themselves, which were seven highly powerful daemons of the ancient world, personal servitors of Aset.

Guardians are remarkably important pillars inside the Asetian family. They are commonly defined by their powerful connection with the Earth and the slowest energy metabolism among vampires, which allows them to fast for long periods of time without feeding or actively manipulating energy, turning out to be a great vampiric asset. This characteristic, combined with their always-present grounding and the inborn ability to create incredible energy shields, grants them a great defensive position among vampires. They are very difficult to drain by non-Asetians and are hardly victimized by energy attacks or any other forms of magick. Scorpions easily change their aura to an unpleasant vibration, so their energies become unattractive to others. This characteristic is another of their innate defensive abilities.

They have the strongest physical connection of the three, manifesting in a very good health and a great immune system, which can only be shacked by energy imbalances. They are the most enduring of the Asetian kind. This great connection with the physical plane can, in some cases, also manifest by increases in weight, a situation that can be balanced by self-control and energy mastery. Although not a definitive characteristic of the lineage, they are commonly not as recognizable by the markedly frail bodies of Serpents.

While this good link with the physical is a very useful characteristic, it is also one of the Guardians' worst problems. Because of their very developed shields and solid grounding, they are the ones with a higher handicap when it comes to interacting with energy, and sometimes with the less sensitivity towards metaphysics in a conscious level, reacting to it most of the times unconsciously. This can, but is not always a characteristic, manifest by poor creativity, skeptical understanding of some mystical subjects, and no close proximity to religious practices, in the times precedent to the awakening.

But even though Guardians are the ones with less inborn abilities to manipulate energy, this does not mean that they cannot become powerful energy practitioners. With dedication and effort, a Guardian can truly master any magickal work, like any other lineage.

Despite this apparent inability from the Guardians, they tend to master the practice of *Tantric Feeding*, in a much more efficient and advanced way than any of the other lineages. Through this practice they easily drain vital energy by that sexual experience, many times without needing to have any physical pleasure of their own. When a real Tantric Feeding state is achieved, the pleasure that the Guardian is giving to the sexual partner is enough for the vampire's needs, feeding from all the high vibrations and energies released by the receiving partner. The pleasure released within these energies is absorbed by the giving Guardian during this type of feeding, and in this way achieving a state where the need to sense physical pleasure of their own is shifted to second place or discarded at all. This is not an easy or basic type of feeding, but an advanced magickal technique that can be practiced by anyone adept at vampiric energy work, especially by those who master sex magick. But despite the magickal training, it is an innate ability from the Guardian lineage, which through this skill, can rely on a more efficient feeding technique towards intense vital energy draining.

Also, they can easily harness vital energy by romantic interaction, but only if it is from someone they love. Behind their shields and energy cloaks Guardians are beings of pure love, who can be positively balanced by the presence of caring and loving feelings in his life. Those are feelings that they do not easily feel by everyone, and many times attaching them to someone forever, when that special soul is found. This makes the Guardians very independent beings, unlike any other of the two lineages. Despite those very few that they appreciate and care about, they easily do not feel the need of interaction, and many times even compassion, towards all others. Even if it is someone close to them on the current incarnation, like a mother or a father. Most of these characteristics might only become obvious and strongly defined after the awakening.

It is curious, since Guardians are many times seen as cold and detached creatures without feelings, but the truth is that in fact they can be very sensitive and caring, but only able to express it towards some select few. To many of the Guardians, love is the engine of life itself, the energy that sustains them and makes them move, adapt and evolve. Nothing makes sense without the presence of that one true love, which they believe in, and all the motivations and actions of life itself are kept to fulfill that one purpose – living with and for the loved one. This dedication easily leads to jealousy and a huge sense of possession, making them far more aggressive and intolerant due to these feelings of belonging and need of control.

With the low energy need experienced by the Asetian Guardians, they do not feed as regularly as the other two lineages. Feeding through small direct drains from their closest partners, to some social situations where they project themselves and impose above others, the Guardians are known to keep their energy reserves to a minimum, without exhibiting any vulnerability, but degrading their sanity slowly. Many times maintaining that situation for long periods of time, with just slow drains from the ambient energy. This manifests clearly in a known difficulty towards change and adaptation from the Guardian lineage. Without the active circulation of new energy in the subtle system, the mind develops attachment mechanisms and does not have enough cycling of energy to set in motion the changes, both internal and external, to adapt to a new condition and in this way accept change itself. So, because of this, changes in the life of a Guardian are usually more troublesome and sometimes cause deep emotional impacts and unbalances due to their own subtle nature.

Elemental energy is an easy empowerment resource for Guardians, since they easily connect with its nature and vibrations, especially the energies related with Earth and Water. This innate connection with the vibrations of nature leads to situations that might be interpreted as attraction by natural scenarios and locations, where the Guardians easily drain high quantities of these energies. In a subtle system that is not used to very high impulses of energy, these massive drains from elemental sources and the urge to feed from it, quickly absorbing it, can lead to emotional peaks and strong sensations during the process.

The low energy metabolism represents the main reason why Guardians are the less sanguinarian among Asetians, rarely blood feeding. Their low energy need combined with their highly developed shields tends to accumulate old energy in their subtle bodies, incrusting inside the meridians and slowing down main Shen Centers, resulting in blockages and energy stagnation. If left without control and energy healing, can easily transform into depression. In worst cases, stagnation centers can start to degenerate, echoing to the physical body, creating tumors and other illnesses. However, this can be applied to all forms of energy stagnation inside the subtle body, human or vampiric, and not just specific to Guardians. The energy stagnation from the Guardians can be set in motion by the higher capacities of Viperines to drain, manipulate and transform energy. Although not as efficiently, Concubines can also help in this situation by the use of their active cycling, breaking the stagnation centers from the Guardians and promoting energy flow.

The powerful energy shields found in this lineage can even reflect in their own skin, since they usually are the less pale from the three lineages. Because of this, they represent the bloodline with less sensibility towards sunlight, which does not mean that it is not really present. Commonly it does not harm their skin as much, nor does it unbalance and block their abilities, as intensely as it would do to a Viperine. But it can still hurt their secondary Shen within their eyes and weaken their powers.

Even though not as critics as Viperines in some situations, the Guardians are very critical towards common society and behaviors that reflect a lack of personality or simple need of integration. They are the *adversaries*, and if enough self-confidence is developed, they will have enough strength to confront anyone, sometimes unpleasantly, regarding their own ideas and thoughts, condemning all that goes along with the rest of the human herd. They feel genuinely disgusted by the surrounding society and are very intolerant towards situations, thoughts and opinions where people act in certain ways just because they are expected to do so. In this way, they have a very decided and strong personality, which can only be shaken by internal unbalances of vital energy within their own subtle system or emotional problems, but usually developing a slowly growing rock-solid persona after the awakening.

Unlike Viperines, Guardians commonly have distinct masculine or feminine energies, usually with a very defined polarity. This gives them a recognizable advantage concerning inner balance, but it also conditions their interpretation and view of things.

The intensity of the Guardians' energy is a hallmark of their lineage, being markedly creatures of high sexuality and an undeniable sensuous essence. However, their actions and emotions can also be fueled by rage and anger, which they easily develop because of their personal subtle anatomy. While these burning feelings can result in strong headaches, laziness, and ill temper, they can also direct these energies towards effective energetic attacks or other dumping options, less exhausting towards themselves. Also because of this, Guardians are usually intolerant with indecisive behaviors, literally taking hand of the issues and simply getting the job finished, in this way being active and efficient.

Guardians, together with Viperines, are the most elitist among the Asetian lineages. This, in many cases, can lead to antisocial behaviors and actual interest in being kept apart from the common, vulgar, society. They, most of all, keep their friendships and relationships to a minimum, only sharing their true Self with a highly elite few, having no interest whatsoever in socializing with the masses or getting integrated. This is highly visible after the awakening. On the other hand, it is common to find more sociable Asetians among Concubines, that possess a far less elitist personality, integrating and dealing a lot better with humans.

Last but not least, Guardians are the most loyal of all Asetians. Dedicating themselves truly and deeply to their cause, they are renown as being the most honorable lineage among vampires, in a way that can only be envied by the human race. This loyalty is kept not only towards their own nature and metaphysical family within the Aset Ka, but very especially in relation to their one true love.

SCARAB
THE LINEAGE OF CONCUBINES

C

Concubines

The Lineage of Concubines is known as the Scarab, a symbol of their highly transformative and adapting nature, along with their characteristically intense cycling and ability to share energy with a great ease.

Being the most common among Asetians, Scarabs are also the most chaotic of the three lineages. This is because of a hallmark in the *concubinic* energy system – their inborn and uncontrollable energy cycling. Concubines are constantly absorbing energy around them and from others, filtering and changing it, to then send it back to the environment. While this is a great quality, since among many things, allows them to be an almost unlimited vampiric energy supply, especially for Viperines with whom they easily connect to a greater depth, also condemns them to great mental and energetic instability. This aspect of their nature makes them valuable donors, being one of the lineage's major qualities, but it also reflects in a far more humanized soul, which in a divine bloodline as the Asetians represents their biggest condemnation.

They, most of all, have the ability to become submissive, controlled, dominated and drained by the ones they connect. This does not mean that they act like that with others, on the contrary, since they can also become easily explosive and uncontrollable by people outside of their most intimate relations, making them not submissive at all for some people.

Because of the energy cycling and consequential easy adaptation to different environments, this can sometimes result in a lack of personality from the Concubines that can be seen as just a consequence of their own energetic nature. The instability resulting from the chaotic cycling of energy manifests most of all in psychological problems, confusion and in some worse cases in a complete loss of the sense of Self. Because of the whole different energies they come in contact with and pass through their system, their subtle body does not retain many of the owner's pure energy, with their unique fingerprint, resulting in a process that works like a sort of energy poisoning by outside human energy. This flood in their internal system by outside polluted energy, many times of a low quality, and not native to their own subtle bodies, completely harasses their mind, many times reaching the point of mental collapse.

To protect themselves from this so notorious tendency of the energy system, Scarabs need to practice energy stabilization techniques and maintain a healthy diet, almost on a daily basis, being essential for their sanity and safety to workout some inner balance, especially energetically and emotionally. Also due to this predisposition, Guardians can have a very positive effect on Concubines, which can, from this relationship or interaction, use their powerful shields to keep them safe from the overflow of energy created by their internal system. Because of this, the development of their own energy shields is a high priority for Concubines, together with the development of a strong personality and a decided, conscious, sense of self, so they can interact with others without getting *drowned* on their energies and feelings.

Cyclical stages in their personality and emotions can be expressed by the alteration of mental phases, as a result of conflicting energies, that would leave the Scarab out of balance and disoriented. This bewilderment within their systems can be experienced by trouble in concentration, inattention and apathy, being possible, in worst cases, to even lead to negligence of the Self. Also, while Concubines tend to have some ease in keeping their physical system stable with the ingestion of small amounts of food, for medium to long periods of time; in an unbalanced energetic state,

this high demanding diet can easily change to a strong urge to feed —
physical food and not energy — in high quantities, trying to compensate for
the emotional instability and lack of vital energy, which in terms of
stabilization and balance does not really work out in the end. In some
extreme cases, this situation can even lead to bulimic patterns.

The Concubines tend to be passionate and obsessive lovers, deeply
connecting to the ones they love and establishing a rooted energy link. This
manifests in heightened jealousy towards the ones they love and a
considerable sense of possession about them. Also, they can easily do
incredible things and assume socially wrong positions and attitudes to
prove dedication to the ones they love. They are a lineage of intense and
obsessive feelings, which is also a usual characteristic of the three Asetian
lineages, under different intensities and forms of manifesting it. The
typically Asetian obsessive patterns towards their loved ones are commonly
seen as something bad by the common human minds and almost invariably
not accepted.

When not referring to the ones they like and care about, concubinic
vampires tend to be manipulative and even creative liars. This will,
depending from their intentions, reflect their true Will, and it is not an
absolute characteristic of the lineage.

Concerning their energy polarity, they parallel with Guardians. Their
energy signatures tend to be masculine or feminine, depending on the
creation of their Ba — soul. However, this energy polarity found in
Concubines is not an asset, unlike the one found in the Guardian lineage.
Their unbalanced psyche and permanent flow of energy tends to confuse
and mix their energy signatures, resulting many times in difficulties to
detect and check the correct polarity of the energy flowing inside their
energy bodies. In real world analysis, this can manifest, for instance, in
confusion related with their sexual preferences.

The ability that Concubines have to be drained without a great loss of
their internal stability, despite being the reason why they become great

donors, of both energy and blood, is also accompanied by an unusual sensation of pleasure and pain when they are aggressively drained. This is something that is many times valued and desired by them, especially in a sexual context. This ability depends on a mechanism, specifically inborn to Concubines, which can be learnt by other lineages. This metaphysical tool lets them rely on energy fuel so they are able to nearly stop feeling some types of pain, for short periods of time. Many times transforming it into pleasure, or just feeding from the energy release by the feelings of physical pain.

The Concubines usually are not very independent beings, needing and valuing a high interaction with many types of people. Because of this, they are the ones that deal better with humans, easily mixing between them and sometimes almost acting like one of them. They are undoubtedly the more social of the Asetian lineages and the less elitist of all. Being also the ones that more regularly do not break their bonds with their biological parents, because of a clear handicap in the sense of awareness towards the true Asetian spirituality and their sacred genesis. The ability to overcome this will depend on the strength of the bond that the Concubine had in the old days with their metaphysical family at the Aset Ka, together with how much they will be capable of fighting against their apparent lack of personality, and dedicate openly to their true nature. Because of this, Guardians and Viperines tend to be great role models to Concubines, which from their honorable and proud example they can find a safe way towards their own enlightenment.

ASETIANISM
The Asetian Tradition

Being an Asetian is far more than embracing a system built upon predatory spirituality or following an ancient religion forgotten in time. It is a tradition based on balance. The underlying foundation of this religion of mysteries has a complex and deep spirituality, but at the same time its backbone depends on very simple and subtle things, making it unique and beautiful, like the tender light of the Violet Flame itself.

The whole system embraces the concept of duality. This means that everything is formed by a double side or face, each opposed and attracted by the other. At some extent similar to the concepts of Yin and Yang, widely used in the oriental philosophies like Taoism, martial arts like Tai Chi

Chuan and even medical and health systems like Traditional Chinese Medicine and Acupuncture.

In Asetianism, these two forces, even though opposed, are always present in every being, object and manifestation. Each one attracts the other, making it complete. There can be no life without both, and this applies to everything, even Gods. A God or Goddess would never be completely good or evil, white or black, or else it would be incomplete. In nature this duality is very easy to observe, since you can watch a magnificent and revitalizing sunset while eating and drinking a myriad of tasty food and drinks that only the Earth provides, and a few hours later being killed by a tremendous earthquake, provided by this same Earth – the forces of nature.

This acceptance of darkness and light is a central point in the Asetian tradition, understanding that only through the acknowledgement of these two forces combined inside every one of us and the cooperation and balance between them, can allow a true fulfillment of the individual as a whole, being complete. Someone that only promotes light, peace, harmony and good feelings, saying he never feels anger or hate and that there are no bad feelings inside his heart, is not complete. He is simply blocking part of himself and not admitting a whole other side of his nature, not fully expressing his own reality and not completely knowing himself, repressing many impulses, thoughts and feelings, resulting in an ultimately intolerant, unbalanced and incomplete being. This also applies to anyone that only promotes violence, anger and darkness, without any embrace of the other side present in their own nature.

The unbalances of the opposing forces present in the living beings and in the nature itself, are commonly the causes of diseases, mental and emotional instabilities, and all sorts of unbalances found everywhere, from a thunder storm to an avalanche or a volcano explosion. Unbalance is the key. These opposing forces are not characterized only by darkness and light. They are everything and everywhere. They can be hot and cold, love and hate. Everything has its own opposing force. Of course Asetianism does not explain an avalanche by a mystical and aware force, since those are easily understandable events under the light of science, but they are nevertheless affected by the universal duality. If a volcano explodes it is because of an unbalance between the uplifting magma and the resistance of the rock preventing it from expanding out of the Earth's crust, in a weak balance played between both, facing the forces compelled by the convection cells of heat in the upper mantle. The same is easily observed on earthquakes and tsunamis. They are the result of unbalances in opposed forces and the natural reaction in trying to regain balance. This applies to everything, and manifests inside ourselves as well, in the constant struggle to balance the unbalanceable. Our whole mind is filled with these unbalances and forces that push us in different ways. So one important goal in Asetianism is to acknowledge these opposing forces in our lives, learn to accept them as a whole and try to balance it for a healthier interaction between mind, body and spirit as a one single organism, actively interacting with the environment with a duality-aware thought and balance in mind.

"For every action, there is an equal and opposite reaction."
- Isaac Newton

In the texts of the Asetian Bible, it becomes clear the dual nature of the Asetians. Not in every single line and concept, but when analyzing the big picture behind it, that hybridization of darkness and light, love and vengeance, creation and destruction, life and death, is present and visible in a very direct form. An Asetian is a being of energy and light, capable of the most honorable and loving acts imaginable, but he is also a creature of darkness and decay, with the power of destruction at his grasp. The acknowledgment of these opposing inner poles of the divine Self, as well as the acceptance of the dark, predatory nature, is a crucial step in the evolution of the Asetian soul. Only that can truly allow an Asetian to wield the extraordinary power that resides hidden and silent within the own soul.

All the obstacles to our success, every challenge to our progress and all the resistance to our personal growth, represent the tides and echoes of evolution itself. Maneuvering these situations, overcoming pain and grief, crashing all our obstacles, is the path of Asetianism. Not always the most obvious choices and direct analysis prove to be the wisest, since only the Gods are able to see all ends.

The most important goal in life is to develop the Self. Not everyone can achieve enlightenment during their current incarnation, but Asetianism promotes, above everything else, evolution. The embrace of the Asetian mysteries and the study of its tradition, just by itself, is a main catalyst of change. This *change* is not something physical or tangible, but a deep manifestation of the Self, not always subtle and many times even in an intense and mysterious way. On a more religious level, Asetianism enhances the adept's spirituality and mind with tools, symbols and magick that allow him to evolve, being a true initiation of the soul. By understanding and accepting his own nature, allied to effective and powerful metaphysical practices, the Asetian finds his true Self and a much clearer reality than the mundane world is willing to offer. In this process, not only the magickal abilities increase exponentially, but it becomes a period of self-discovery, with the long-gone past of the soul slowly unveiling behind the veil of other lives, uncovered by the glimpse of the ethereal matter that covers the Akashic records, where all life is stored.

The understanding of the mysteries hidden in the past is a powerful key to evolution and self-development. In this way, past-life work is a major practice of the tradition, working under very distinct techniques and using advanced metaphysical tools to achieve clarity, insight and accurate results. Since Asetianism itself is a very ancient mystical tradition, with many mysteries still lost in time waiting to be unfolded, it is only but obvious that intuitive work applied in a past-life research context is of high importance. While the vast majority of this metaphysical work is directed to the knowledge of Kemet – Ancient Egypt – and the well established lives of the Asetians during this period, from the highly ancient Sep Tepy to the later dynastic periods, it is not out of the subject to research other eras and societies in different timeframes. Many Asetians have been scattered, lost in time and space, being apart from the Aset Ka Order for long periods of time, because of a myriad of reasons and situations. This has led to diversity. With Asetians incarnating under so many different cultures and following such different paths along the way, that has eventually enriched the global Asetian knowledge repositories, giving the Aset Ka a much more global understanding of worldwide metaphysics rather than exclusively the work and knowledge of the Egyptians.

By this we can understand that the concept of reincarnation and past lives is a major anchor in the Asetian knowledge, being a tradition with roots based on a common shared past in Ancient Egypt, with a doctrine that has developed and evolved over time, getting increasingly complex and mature but always keeping and ferociously protecting its own sacred genesis and Kemetic foundation, along with its very intense and profound spirituality. In fact, the concept of reincarnation is so deeply rooted in Asetianism that most of the Asetians would say that it really is not a belief, since they do not accept it out of faith and scriptures, but more of an unshakable truth, in which they do not need to believe... they simply know it exists. After all, they are the ones who have lived and remembered.

"I have been given eternity without limit.
Behold, I am the heir of Eternity,
to whom have been given everlastingness."
- Egyptian Book of the Dead

All this cultural background constantly bringing the Asetian mind to its own past metaphysical practices in Egypt and the entwined Kemetic religious experience could only manifest in a tradition highly connected to an ancient religion that became extinct thousands of years ago. These ties to the complex and vast Kemetic religion, easily found in Asetianism, are not simple surface concepts, but deep mysteries of the world, that tells us about the eternal travel of the soul, and that can be found scattered by tiny bits in almost every concept of the tradition and in every theological

Asetian text since the old days. One of the most obvious and direct ties to Kemeticism is the Asetian Cosmogony, which can be parallel with the Egyptian theology on almost every level. Even when a true connection cannot be readily established, a deeper study of the text and enlightenment into the Asetian symbolism will echo intensely into our inner cores, reflecting many of these parallels with the lost Egyptian beliefs, telling us tales of the past and unfolding many mysteries from the beginning of times.

In modern Asetians this connection with the *Neteru* – the Kemetic word for deities – can be seen manifested in distinct ways. Despite the global devotion and love for the Founder of the Asetianism – Aset – not every Asetian maintains a relevant relation with the rest of the pantheon. While some keep a more purist Kemetic faith, more in like with the religion lived and practiced by the people of Ancient Egypt, others keep a more strictly Asetian approach, only maintaining ties to the tradition lived in secret on the Aset Ka temples of the old days and sometimes almost neglecting the traditional faith more widely spread throughout the common people. This apparent variety in the Asetian religious practices reflect a lot more than a coincidence, but actually the faith followed by them in their first incarnations in Ancient Egypt. While some adepts were closer to the Elders, dwelling more deeply into the inner and obscure mysteries of the Asetians found at the elitist temples of the Aset Ka, other practitioners were not this close to the sources of the tradition or not so highly scholar about it. Sometimes keeping ties with the traditions and beliefs of the rest of their families and friends, resulting in an amalgam of practices, mixing parts of the traditional Kemetic faith with the obscure concepts, metaphysics and magick of Asetianism. It is important, however, to keep in mind that during this period, like all others in which the influence of the Aset Ka was notorious, following the Asetian tradition and their magickal teachings was something to be highly proud of, sometimes even generating jealousy and disputes among friends of the followers, something that was certainly not promoted by the Aset Ka Order. Most of the times, these conflicts occurred from the Asetian followers and Disciples that, despite not being initiated into the inner mysteries, were not even part of the Order itself. In fact, only a very small share of the Disciples and Asetianists were true members of the Aset Ka, which membership was not only highly elitist but also very difficult to accomplish, and only made accessible to the most devoted and honorable followers.

The Asetian history is full of conflicts, obstacles and wars that eventually pushed the Aset Ka Order out of Egypt and into Europe. However, it is important to keep in mind that many of these wars that eventually interfered with the Asetian path during history were mundane, social and political, and not something in which the Asetians actively intervened. The conflicts in which this was the case, were surely not wars that the Aset Ka started out of a quest for fame and glory, but arising from the effect that the Asetians usually cause in people, especially from religiously-obsessed sects in society, where the profound knowledge of the Asetians and their understanding of nature and metaphysics were always an obvious flag, signalizing those who hunger for power for an immediate destruction and eternal silencing of the Asetian bloodline.

The dark tradition of Aset was always a problem to the human mind, which does not want the knowledge of the Gods, but seeks only for their power. This remains true until today, and will endure, but so will the Asetians. The Children of Aset cannot be destroyed. This was Her gift. Immortality and everlastingness.

"Our deeds still travel with us from afar,
and what we have been makes us what we are."
- George Eliot

Asetians are not simply a group of followers of the same tradition of mysteries. They are many times seen as a family. This was much more evident in the ancient times, where the group was very close, but it is a link that still endures. The ability that the Asetians have to choose their own parents and places on which they opt to incarnate strengthens this link with their metaphysical family. This can, in some cases, promote a sense of detachment from their biological families, which can be seen as a vessel to the physical realm, and not really the seed of their own ancient life. This aspect is far more complex to understand to a non-Asetian mind, where the parents are usually revered with a feeling of owing them for their life. Since most of the humans cannot actively choose their parents and make a more conscious option towards their next incarnation during the in-between lives stage, they also cannot achieve enlightenment in such an easy way towards this specific subject like a being that has control over their own rebirth cycle. This does not mean in any way that the Asetians should mistreat their families. It just means that they treat them however they feel they deserve, and not with any fear or extra respect by something that they are not entitled – their life. Certainly, many of these concepts, knowledge and feelings are heightened after the awakening, and in some fewer cases it only starts to manifest after it. Most of the Asetians know their true origins and genesis, and that comes from someone of the Asetian family or even a deity – Aset – in the case of the Primordials. Because of this acknowledgment, the Asetians commonly consider the Aset Ka their true family, and nurture for them a profound respect and intimate bond, usually far more deep and true than for the current biological family found in this life. All these connections that resist the break of death and endure through many lifetimes, result in a sense of honor towards their Asetian family and true deep feelings that also represent a sense of loyalty seen in the Aset Ka like it cannot be found elsewhere in our era.

Asetianism promotes understanding on a raw level. In every incarnation, the Asetian fights to achieve self-realization. This is a slow and constant process of discovery, growth and adaptation. The constant seek and conquering of his goals, in the life of an Asetian, promotes a dynamic expansion of his consciousness, in a permanent cycle of rebirth. The profound self-realization that the Asetian seeks empowers him with joy and happiness. These feelings of happiness and profound inner peace are not only promoted through the evolution of the Self and in the realization found from it, but also is a deep feeling that awaits behind the void to those that, like the Children of Aset, have felt the sacredness of the divine spark. Asetians have tasted the nectar of immortality. They are beings of energy, empowered with the essence of the Violet Flame. They celebrate life, and live it deeply. Asetianism is about loving Aset, unconditionally embracing life and honoring the divine within.

In the quest for balance that every Asetian undergoes in every single lifetime, there is a need to achieve a subtle harmony between the three main aspects of its current existence: the mind, the body and the spirit. Only a wise symmetry between these interlaying factors can help in the promotion of a sane and healthy life. However, that is a very hard condition to achieve, especially for a vampiric creature, who's own nature promotes unbalances, chaos and change. Instabilities in any of those factors echo to all the others, which is why a weak spirit easily promotes disease and why troubles in the mind produce the exact same thing. Everything is interconnected, and unbalance in something ends up harming the other layers of existence. Stability and self-control must be valuable goals to every Asetian, helping him along his way, step by step, towards enlightenment. This later stage of the Asetian development is a slow, dangerous and obscure path of self-discovery, which unfolds in the mist of each lifetime. Each of these lives being a further evolutive step in the quest for knowledge and enlightenment, along the eternal cycle of rebirth.

The quest for enlightenment as an ultimate but not definitive goal for an Asetian is a path that embraces a magnitude of things. One of the major pillars in this pursuit is knowledge. Through it, an Asetian finds his true Self and embraces his own nature, develops his assets, abilities and in a very simple way, ultimately develops himself. Knowledge is a very important tool in the development of the initiate, being also a widely respected asset among the Asetians. While this knowledge refers to a myriad of subjects and overall culture, the metaphysical and occult consciousness and insight is kept on the top of this pyramid, being commonly used as a guideline and important factor to distinguish between the evolved and the stagnated, or for the more aggressive and elitist to distinguish the inferior creatures from the superior ones.

Development and enlightenment is a slow and enduring process of the Asetian journey through life. This metaphysical initiation is a system of transmutation. By this pure and deep change, it is meant that the Asetian achieves to alter in form, appearance and nature, which is a manifestation of the force of the Violet Flame itself. This transmutation, deeply connected with the vampiric birth, represents the alchemical nature of the Asetian soul, ever changing and eternal. According to this, we can establish the Asetians as the alchemists of the soul, creators and destroyers, catalysts of change and evolution, with the power to transform *lead* into *gold*. Asetians are the givers of life, the pillars of the subtle existence, owners of the breath of immortality. Actually, alchemy is so connected with Ancient Egyptian practices and knowledge that even the word has its roots in the Arabic *al-kimiya*, and meaning *from Kemet*, literally symbolizing *The art from Kemet*. So the real alchemy is a legacy of the knowledge of the ancients, a central practice and expertise of the Asetians, not as the distorted alchemy of the Middle Ages, that would later give birth to modern Chemistry, but as the Kemetic art of spiritual transformation and development.

It has been mentioned that magick and energy manipulation can be seen as central practices among the adepts of Asetianism. However, a universal tool, used by all Asetians, is meditation. Through the act of meditating an individual can accomplish multiple things, from energizing and relaxing himself, to more advanced magick like astral traveling, energy projection and Akashic regression. Let alone, meditative work is under high esteem among Asetians, being both a common and a regular part of their lives, like eating or drinking. From advanced techniques, spiritual and religious practices, to contemplative meditation, all Asetians find in meditation a valuable tool to their inner development and self-discovery. In fact, meditation is such a regular practice among Asetians that it only gets surpassed by energy work. Being themselves beings of energy and vibration, and consciously acknowledging that during their lives, the interaction with energy and its manipulation is an everyday and constant practice, which many accomplish on a low level without giving any special thought about it. Living in a layered energy world, surrounded by its forces and constantly interacting with them on its many levels, is an aspect of the life of any Asetian. This permanent and definitive connection with the subtle energy is such a hallmark in Asetianism that it even defines their basic nature, commonly expressed by the word *vampire*. As vampires, this energy bond is more than a way of life and an ability, but a necessity. Only through it the whole system of the vampire can be kept stable. It is a subtle condition of the soul itself.

It is crucial for any Asetian to acknowledge the true nature of their vampirism, along with the huge distinction between fiction and reality. A vampire is a whole world more than a simple being that craves for energy. The meaning behind it is very complex and deep, representing a very special immortal being bound to the subtle existence. A creature of magick and power. Most of all... the Asetian is a divine soul incarnated. It is always important to keep present that crucial distinction between what being a vampire truly means and what common people think vampires are. The Asetians gave birth along the ages to a myriad of vampiric mythologies and lore, but a vampire must perceive the reasons behind the existence of those concepts, that in many cases are no more than imagined stories of the human mind that cannot comprehend the true essence behind an Asetian vampire.

As an esoteric tradition, Asetianism is against futile cultivation of the ego and ego worship, however they do not deny the ego as part of their own nature. An Asetian does not neglect the pleasures of life while incarnated. Actually they enforce life and pleasure, because together they are allies to self-development and achievement. An uncontrolled and over-demanding ego can condemn anyone's evolution, but its undervaluation is against our own nature and definitely malignant in the end. Why people should not use the clothes they like, opt for different kinds of food, make love embracing its pleasure, decorate their homes how they like even if guided by their inner egocentric appeal, read different books and delight with world's art, listening to music? It is all about ego and pleasure. Should we deny that? Never. We are here to develop and evolve spiritually, but we are also to embrace all life has to offer. However, this does not mean that we should give a major importance to our ego and be guided by it. Magick, mysticism and occultism should never be used to fulfill our ego and inner desires to prove we are better and more powerful than others. Magick does not serve that purpose, ever, and no Asetian would practice magick for amusement of others and feed his inner ego, nor will he ever give a magickal demonstration just to prove he can or that he is able to. That is completely against evolution and a lack of respect for the essence of magick itself.

Asetianism being a dark tradition, involving such taboo themes as predatory spirituality and so many feared concepts and knowledge such as obscure high magick and first-class energy manipulation, together with the deeply introspective and meditative practices, the Asetian tradition is more than always seen with a bit of fear and intolerance, mainly because of its apparent *evil* nature and inhumane practices, by those who do not fully understand it or aren't knowledgeable enough to intelligently comment on it. However, despite being vampires, Asetians do not identify themselves as daemons. The whole concept of a modern vampire is just an archetype of darkness and predatory nature. It does not impose any relation with the medieval monstrosity of the bloodsucking vampire beast or with the modern fictionalized view of it as flying hero.

Can you imagine a so-called modern vampire astral traveling inside and in the surroundings of the Taj Mahal, jogging on the Great Wall, sleeping in the King's Chamber inside the Great Pyramid of Khufu or deeply meditating inside the Temple of Philae? Well... I can certainly imagine that from an Asetian vampire.

Despite being an established tradition with a strong identity of its own, Asetianism promotes comparative religious study and research on different cultures, knowledge and traditions. This is true because the Asetians believe that the truth is out there to be found, and knowledge is not something to be preached or forced, especially when it comes to spiritual matters and religious truth. In this way, the cultural development and learning of other philosophies, traditions and practices is something that is always encouraged inside the Aset Ka, and kept under a great esteem as a valuable asset to the initiate. Through this, an adept does not only gain a considerable amount of knowledge and information, helping to solidify his own tradition and beliefs, clarifying the inner initiatory path of the Asetian soul, but also empowers him with a great cultural background that works as a resource to powerful social interaction and enlightened discussions. Not only because of this, but also helped by it, a fully awakened and trained Asetian is someone that is proud of his own knowledge and expertise, and that can keep an interesting and intelligent conversation with almost anyone, under a myriad of situations and subjects, being highly knowledgeable at a wealth of information. While this is a major asset to anyone, it can also be seen as a tool. Vampires are experts in manipulation, induction and pretending, so their cultural advantage can easily be used to gain a strategic position among a debate and other kinds of situations. This is something that if combined with efficient energy work, can prove to be a state-of-the-art magickal tool, and be seen as a great ability, or a great danger.

Magick represents a basal stronghold of the Asetian existence. They study the essence of magick throughout the millennia, recreating it and developing it. In a way, Asetians are the keepers of the magickal knowledge of the ancients. Magick represents a crucial part of their lives, and without it, nothing would make any sense. This is true since life itself is magical, and it is empowered by nature, that is a dynamic and powerful magickal force. Asetians acknowledge the importance of nature, its vitality and power, valuing it as an irreplaceable treasure that should be cared and esteemed. It is hard for an Asetian mind to comprehend the atrocities that the human species constantly do to the precious gift of nature that was freely given for them to cherish. They consider this as disrespectful and a shame to the whole human race, from which they do not nourish much respect.

Still on the subject of metaphysics, working with minerals is one of the first techniques that any Asetian learns to master, sometimes connecting with this form of subtle energy even prior to the awakening. Minerals are exceptional magickal tools, not only amplifying the projected vital energy in different ways according to their own nature, composition and characteristics, but also emanating a very stable energy field of their own, proving to be great resources for that specific energy type. Because of this reason, it is common for an Asetian to use a special mineral connected with his own energy, as a talisman or even as a wand. This habit is not something new, but a practice that still endures from the days lived in Kemet, where minerals were highly valued because of their magickal properties and metaphysical characteristics. Despite the common use of these tools among Asetians, their usability is not simple. Implicating not only effective energy cleansing techniques, but especially relying on a sacred procedure of synchronization and attunement of the specific mineral using skills and techniques of energy manipulation that date back to the Asetian genesis. Some of these procedures are still maintained secret and considered sacred knowledge, practiced by an *Encantatum*, usually a higher priest from the Asetian Temple. Although a huge variety of mineral species is valued by the Asetians, there is one that is considered more than just a tool, but something special. This mineral is known as Amethyst, a special variety of Quartz, composed by tetrahedrons of Silicon Dioxide (SiO_2) and Manganese, with a characteristic violet and purple color. Despite the metaphysical qualities inherent to this mineral, the Amethyst has a very particular connection to the Asetians, with its natural energy field easily connecting with their subtle body and forging an energy link. This is true because this mineral is a highly magnifier of the energy vibration found in the Violet Flame. Also because of this, the Asetians tend to easily project high intensity beams of vital energy through this mineral, especially if it is attuned and shaped in particular forms, according to sacred geometry and crystallography, becoming far more efficient when it comes to amplifying energy. But not only magick represents a key into the underlying mysteries of the Asetian tradition. The academic and practical study of the occult and the unknown are intrinsic principals of the Asetian nature, making the Asetian Elders true scholars of the metaphysical, occult history and esoteric knowledge, being highly erudite on this obscure wisdom.

Dream work and its analysis is a regular practice among Asetian initiates, that rely on the altered states of consciousness achieved during the period of sleep to access different realities and walk into more subtle realms. The world of dreams opens the door to the unconscious mind in a more direct way than any other method, being highly indicated in a process of discovery of the Self. But through this inner tunnel of our own unconscious, the road does not just lead to the internal reality of the dream realm, but also to a far broader place, into the astral plane itself. In a procedure common to the practices of Shamanism, it is possible to plunge into our inner realms and through this state access the outer reality of the higher planes, like the astral and the etheric. Despite this form of projecting the soul, there is still useful potential to be harnessed during dream work. Like it is possible to open a door to the macrocosm from the inside of our microcosm, it is also possible to access hidden knowledge from the etheric realms, like our own link to the Akashic Records, being a great tool to integrate past-life work and passive regression techniques. Using dream work to render information on past lives can prove to be a great asset in global past-life work, allowing for the uncovering of some information in greater detail and sometimes-lost pieces of information that can be precious in the long run. To anyone developing serious dream work, an organized registration of the data is a very valuable option. This is usually done in the form of a dream journal, or Asetian Memories booklet, like the one used inside the Aset Ka. With this simple tool, it will be easier to analyze and correlate different experiments and achieved results, and at the same time it works as an anchor point that promotes and solidifies the remembering mechanism used in the process.

In the end, despite the importance of all magickal practices and metaphysical work developed by the Asetian along his path and development, his inner religion is the mysterious backbone to his own whole existence. The lack of religiosity from vampires is a common erroneous assumption found in modern literature, proliferated by the vampire lifestyle subculture, which found in the immortal predator a powerful archetype for their weaknesses but were not ready to embrace the full spirituality that came with it. The vampiric path is interconnected with a profound sense of divineness allied to a strong devotion that surpasses faith. This strong religiosity from the real vampires is supported by a profound system of spirituality, that is not accessible to just anyone and certainly is out of the scope to the common mind. The concepts of no attached religion to vampirism and the lack of divinity or deity manifestations in their philosophies is just a disguised form of modern Satanism, adapted to the vampire archetype, being just a modern concept that has nothing to do with the real vampiric spirituality. The commercial scene of pseudo-vampires, that have found in their lifestyle and role-playing concepts a way to strive and proliferate, has become in many cases the true lack of elitism, culture, spirituality and profound knowledge that the real vampires themselves have fought to keep inviolable pillars of the vampire community, that still linger today in orders like the Aset Ka, since times immemorial. That is one of the reasons why the Kemetic Order prefers to be kept aside of the so-proclaimed modern vampire communities, to retain its own spirituality and ideals out of the scope of these new-age subcultures, maintaining its integrity and personality, while keeping the religious mysteries of the ancient and magickal knowledge accessible only to those who honor that same knowledge and honestly dedicate to the path of Aset, the mother of the Asetians, the initiator of the vampires, the creator of the first-born... the *Holy Mater*.

Asetianism, as a sacred immemorial tradition founded by the Gods, embodied within itself a highly powerful system of magick, a spiritual path to immortality and a profound religion of mysteries. However, this tradition was not lived only by the Asetians, but was also embraced by human Disciples, followers and allies of the Asetians, as well as by the Children of Anubis, known within the tradition as The Keepers. All of these people forged a secret alliance, shared their love and energies, and were ultimately part of the stronghold and metaphysical engine that empowered the mighty Asetian Empire.

DJEHUTYS
A JOURNEY OF TIME

jehutys is the common name for the Asetian Eras. From the Kemetic God Thoth – Djehuty in Ancient Egyptian – controller of time and creator of writing, it is the term we use to define different temporal intervals in our spiritual history. Each of these Djehutys is characterized by a specific formula of religious spirituality and thought patterns. The different Djehutys correlate and parallel with different markings, steps and time measures of different religions and occult sciences.

Currently we are entering in the *Djehuty of the Serpent*, which started around the year 2000, but we are still in a very early stage of its transition, where the vast majority of generalized thought is still stuck in the previous Djehuty.

Before the current one, there are known three earlier Djehutys: the *Djehuty of the Scorpion*, the *Djehuty of the Hawk* and the *Djehuty of the Crocodile*.

The Sting of the Sacred Scorpion

The **Djehuty of the Scorpion**, highly connected with Aset, is what we call the Age of the Gods, or *Sep Tepy*, the Egyptian words for *First Time*. It is a huge timeframe that spans from the beginning of times to around 5000 BC.

This is the age where the Asetians trace back their roots, where Aset gave birth to the three Primordials and when the transformations of the Elders occurred. It was the time when the Gods themselves walked this earth, harnessed their powers and energies, and left the knowledge later to be used by the Egyptian people, to create the most advanced civilization the world has ever seen, in terms of culture, medicine, architecture, engineering, science and of course... magick.

It was also during this Djehuty and entering into the next that the period and battles known as the Epic Wars took place, with their fights for supremacy, power and honor. It was the age of the foundation of the Aset Ka Order and the forge of the great Asetian Empire. It was a time of magick and temples, when the lands of Kemet were not as desertified as they are now. The Sahara was still beginning to form, and part of those lands belonged to the rule of Seth, in contrast with the flourishing and advanced cities along the Nile, that were part of the Asetian Empire. In those days, the Aset Ka had one of the biggest armies in the world, but they could even be outnumbered by the Sethian hordes together with their allies from the South. However, war was never about numbers, and the colossal Epic Wars would come to an end under the power of a much smaller army, but a far greater force, known as the Imperial Guard, the most devastating force that any battle has ever witnessed on Earth. This was Aset's private army, and not only highly trained Asetians were part of those forces, but some older creatures... daemons of the ancient world. Actually these events are even related with the name of the Djehuty itself, since the Imperial Guard was known for their designs and engraves of a stinging Scorpion on their shields and swords, reason that led the people to call it *The Scorpion Army*. This is directly connected with the personal guard of Aset, composed of seven daemons, the *Seven Scorpions*.

Even though the battles of the Sep Tepy were a strong mark of this age and a stain in the history of the Aset Ka, this period was far more vast and peaceful than what it might seem. It was also a time of development, growth and achievement. The harmonious periods inside of the Sep Tepy era were of major beauty, peace and prosperity. The Asetian Empire was a golden reign, which brought the civilization up from anarchy and primitive societies to the advanced world of the Egyptian civilization, achieving such a high level of prosperity that mankind alone would never accomplish. A sacred age forgotten in time, the only era when Gods and men were together.

The Flight of the Royal Hawk

The **Djehuty of the Hawk**, that achieved its peak around 2500 BC, was characterized by a matriarchal society around the globe, of Mother Earth and of the religions centered in the cult of the Goddess, where the woman was respected as a pillar of society and the center of life. It is a time where the human knowledge in some cultures was sometimes so restricted that the pregnancy of a woman and the birth of a child were not always seen related to the sexual act between man and woman, reason by which the woman alone was seen as responsible for all the creation and prosperity of the species. At the same time, the Earth was seen as a mother and female to many tribes, and it was from this same Earth that all food came, allowing for all beings to grow, live and prosper. So it was also Mother Earth that assured life and creation. Many of these thoughts about the divinity of the woman and her power in society were also an indirect reflex of the vast influence of the Asetian Empire of the last Djehuty, with their spiritual foundation that was ever so respectful towards woman and where they always represented a central backbone in Asetianism.

This was also the time of Pharaonic Egypt, and the period where the Asetians gave the throne of Kemet to the humankind, perpetuating their now spiritual empire forever in the shadows and in secret. The Pharaohs identified themselves with Horus, the first-borne Asetian, as a representation of the majesty of their ancient empire, and as a remembrance of the times where Egypt was ruled by Gods, and Horus was the King within their royal family. Being here also a connection with the name of the Djehuty, where Horus was many times paralleled with a mighty Hawk, and this was the age of the Pharaohs after all, the end of Aset's direct rule and passing of the leadership to Horus. During part of this new Egyptian period of men, there were dynasties that were again ruled back by Asetians, but this time in secret to most of the people and as a result of their powers over the reincarnation cycles. This was not a constant or permanent rule, and most of the details are still kept with great secrecy in terms of modern history.

In the beginnings of this historical stage, there were also periods of political instability, since after the Sep Tepy and the Asetian leadership, the Egyptian empire ceased to be a unified force. In these times of decreased prosperity, Egypt was controlled by different powers, and many times divided into Upper and Lower Egypt. Being unified again under one single force by the pharaonic power of the House of Horus, that unified Upper and Lower Egypt back into one single kingdom, as in the old days of the Sep Tepy, and became the time scholarly known in our days as dynastic Egypt.

In this Djehuty of the woman, the magickal formula assented on the power of the Goddesses and endured until around 500 AD, by the time that the Philae Temple in Egypt, once a powerful religious stronghold of the Asetians, was officially closed down by the Byzantine emperor Flavius Justianus, having its priesthood chased down and the noble art of the hieroglyphs forgotten, in part forever...

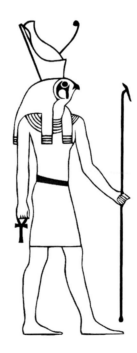

The Haunting of the Treacherous Crocodile

By this time, the magickal formula of global thought was beginning
to change. We were shifting to the **Djehuty of the Crocodile**, usually
paralleled with a corrupted version of the theology of Osiris, because of the
religious formula of this age, coincident with the medieval ages and which
religious roots expand until today. It is the time of the implementation of
the patriarchal societies, of the valor of men, physical strength and of the
warrior. Was the passage to the leadership of Kings and Clergy, unlike the
older Djehutys in the Kemetic society, in which existed powerful kingdoms
under the rule of a female Pharaoh and many temples had high priestesses
and priests, in contrast with the pure masculine governments and exclusive
male clergy of the new Djehuty that was being born. It was the age of the
usurpation of the female importance to second plan, now being seen as a
vehicle to the proliferation of the species and not as center of life. Because
now man had discovered the importance of his seed to create life inside the
female body, and the spiritual focus of global thought shifted from the
planet Earth to the star Sun. The preoccupation of mankind stopped being
the maintenance of the species and started to be the perception that death
was an uncontrollable and inviolable consequence of all life. The Sun itself
died everyday and, like all the animals and plants, humans also had their
own final destiny determined at birth.

It was during this period that the monotheistic religions started to
expand and flourish – like Judaism, Christianity and Islam. In many places
around the world, the new Gods started to parallel with the basic Osirian
model, where a male divinity died and was later resurrected.[6] Most of this
newly created divine archetypes paralleled with the Osirian formula, where
Osiris, God of Living, is murdered by his brother Seth, and then he is given
eternal life by the powers of Isis, ruling forever in the Duat, land of the
dead. In the case of the Christian mythology, the bases are so adapted from
the Osirian model that we have a young savior being unfairly killed, a
woman that cries for his death and looks for him, ending in a final
resurrection, clearly copied from the life-giving powers of Isis. In fact, these

new cults became so popular, that even started to demand adherence to them, so that some chance of salvation was even possible from that omnipotent God, and since then the different currents of monotheism became the most influent religious systems of the last 2000 years.

This period connected with the Crocodile, the beast of the Nile, was one of the darkest times in the Asetian history, when the Order of Aset Ka was most weak and fragile. It was an era of Sethian dominion, when the Red Order of Seth spiritually imposed its empire around the globe, under the shadows of his inner powers and astonishing secrecy of the ages.

The Awakening of the Ancient Serpent

Arriving at the **Djehuty of the Serpent**, a new and unexpected chain of thought and growing spirituality began to appear within the most evolved human thought. We had arrived at what is called the *New Age*. The old religions were decadent and have achieved a point of no return, even though they still do not accept that reality very much, but nonetheless feel it deep within.

Some beings started to better understand the nature of divinity and their true origins, beginning to evolve spiritually, accepting change and transformation as a process of enlightenment. Now it was not the Sun dying every day, the vision was more complex; it died every night but was also reborn every morning. And so life would not vanish forever, people also died to be reborn. Death was just another essential phase of everyone's personal evolution. The fear of extinction and death cult of the old religions was now being replaced by a new and positive spirituality, less sick and in a form of a cult of life and rebirth, which slowly begins to replace the generalized fear of death that was so typical in the *Djehuty of the Crocodile.* The decadent and corrupted monotheistic religions that reigned through the dark ages of the last Djehuty were now being broken down by the truth of the ancient polytheistic traditions, that had for a very long time understood the reality of reincarnation and celebrated it as one of the true mysteries of life itself. A sacred religious mystery that draws its roots back to the beginning of times, to the traditions of Ancient Egypt and the spiritual knowledge of the Asetians. However, a large part of the world's population is still stagnant in the old Djehuty, being a phenomenon that always happens when there is a change and transformation to a new era and the birth of a new spiritual formula. The old religions and thought patterns show some resistance to change and implementation of the new knowledge. But evolution knows no limits or frontiers, and eventually all the roots from the old and rotten *Djehuty of the Crocodile* will be removed and surpassed by the young, fresh and powerful *Djehuty of the Serpent*: the time of individual thought and spiritual evolution without fears or restrictions, the era where life is closer to its true divine nature.

It was also during the beginning of this new era that living vampires decided to set forth and come out from the shadow. Unfortunately this attitude is leading, in many situations, to a popularization of vampirism, something that happened not very long ago to some neo-pagan movements. This vulgarization of the predatory occultism, being anti-vampiric per se, is one of the many reasons why this book is also reaching the general public. Among the scarce literature about real vampirism, only very few public texts and works can actually be taken seriously in consideration by the occult society. In this way, the partial disclosure of the foundations of the Asetian tradition to a more broad audience will help interested students and scholars of predatory spirituality to differentiate modern vampiric texts with erroneous concepts from real and valuable material. The vampiric path has always been an elitist and secretive one, and while the new freedom of information that this Djehuty brought into the occult sciences is a very positive phenomenon to the evolution of many, the mysteries and profound spirituality of the predatory traditions cannot be lost or transformed into popular occultism at the easy grasp of all.

To the Asetians, this new Djehuty that draws its force from the archetype of Horus – one of the three Primordials of the bloodline – is also a time of awakening. Some Asetians have not even reincarnated during the period of the *Djehuty of the Crocodile*, and to the ones that did, those were dark times, in an age of secrecy and strife. Those were the days where the Aset Ka was more weakened in its whole history and when the Asetian family got scattered. Many Asetians were lost in time, and reborn far from their eternal metaphysical family. And only now, in this new era of the Serpent, the new age of the Asetians, they are reawakening and finding their true Self back again, coming closer to their long forgotten Order of Aset Ka and reuniting with their true bloodline – the Asetians. This is the new era of this world, the *Second Age of Vampires*, the reawakening of the ancient Serpent from its long sleep through the ages. This truly is the age of the Asetians rising...

"*All that is gold does not glitter,*
Not all those who wander are lost;
The old that is strong does not wither,
Deep roots are not reached by frost.

From the ashes a fire shall be woken,
A light from the shadows shall spring;
Renewed shall be blade that was broken:
The crownless again shall be King."

- John Ronald Reuel Tolkien

WATCHTOWERS
ELEMENTALS OF THE PHYSICAL UNIVERSE

The Watchtowers are the four guardians of the natural world within the Physical Universe. These elementals, commonly summoned during ritual work and many times used for protection in ceremonial magick, or to affect a specific existence inside this reality, are of some importance in the Asetian magickal workings and system. These four entities guard and control the four elements of the Physical Universe – Air, Fire, Water and Earth. They are powerful ethereal beings, part of nature itself, commonly known as elementals.

On the Asetian tradition, the four elements are part of the Kemetic theology and can be understood behind the concept of the *Four Sons of*

Horus. Each of these elementals that are entrusted with the control and mastery of one of the four natural elements is part of the essence of Horus.

In a more mythological approach, Horus was the ruler that the Gods entrusted leadership on Earth when they left their physical form at the end of the Sep Tepy period. Horus was a beloved king in the ancient Asetian Empire, and his divine essence forever endured around all of us in many forms – from the great shifting powers of the Water to the destroyer hotness of Fire, from the subtle and invisible Air to the fertile and life sustaining Earth.

Each of these powerful elementals is also connected with a specific cardinal point, according to the way they can be summoned, and they also manifest in a particular color on a subtle energy level, which are described in the following page. A specific deity protects each of the watchtowers, being also connected with the form of the Canopic Jars – funerary vases crafted by the ancient Egyptians and used to keep the organs of the mummified corpses of the dead. Each of the four jars kept a specific organ, related with the son of Horus – elemental – that was protecting it.

These beings are not creatures of good or evil. They are above those concepts and definitions, and can be summoned by the practitioner as protection during ritual and even bound to our will if enough power is achieved. However, they cannot be fully controlled, because of their chaotic and dynamic nature. They are part of the foundations of this universe.

Duamutef

The first elemental is that of the East, with control over the powers of Air. It is the canopic jar that contained the stomach and is represented with a head of a jackal. Yellow is the dominant color and the goddess Neith protects it.

Imset

The second elemental is that of the South, with control over the powers of Fire. It is the canopic jar that contained the liver and is represented with a human head. Red is the dominant color and the goddess Isis protects it.

Qebehsenuf

The third elemental is that of the West, with control over the powers of Water. It is the canopic jar that contained the intestines and is represented with a head of a hawk. Blue is the dominant color and the goddess Serket protects it.

Hapi

The fourth elemental is that of the North, with control over the powers of Earth. It is the canopic jar that contained the lungs and is represented with a head of a baboon. Green is the dominant color and the goddess Nephthys protects it.

ASETIAN MANIFESTO

To become an Asetian is to die and be reborn.

To forget all you have learned and learn all you have forgotten.

To be an Asetian is to be blessed with everlasting Love.

Is to be cursed by a never-ending thirst for perfection.

An Asetian is a fierce warrior, a faithful lover and an eternal concubine. Having the power of the Pharaoh, the discipline of the Samurai, the knowledge of the Wizard and the commitment of the Geisha.

Kemet is our Holy Land. The genesis of our immortal Ba.

The Tao is Knowledge. Power is through Blood.

Our Ka is sacred.

Our essence is the storm raindrops in the ocean of mankind, the winds that blow on their faces and the quakes that shake the very foundations of their ground.

We are the children of the Gods.
We are the Cursed Ones and the Blessed Ones.

We live in Secret. We live in Silence. And we live Forever...

PART TWO

METAPHYSICS
VIBRATIONAL MAGICK

SUBTLE ENERGY

E nergy can be defined as the metaphysical fluid that constitutes the subtle field that surrounds everything and it is present in every living being. The concept is found in many different contexts and cultures, like the Ki in Japanese martial arts, the Chi in traditional Chinese medicine, the Prana in the Hindu religion from India, the Mana from the Polynesian culture, the Ether in Alchemy, among many others. Basically, energy is an ethereal fluid that manifests in different types and conditions, under a complex spectrum of vibrations and frequencies.

The notion that this kind of energy is only present in the living beings, in the form of an energy field – most commonly known as aura – is not entirely correct. The comprehension of this concept can be better understood under the Ancient Egyptian definitions of Ba and Ka, widely used by Asetians. They are both Ancient Egyptian words and each one can be represented by a single hieroglyph, being in fact two major pillars of the Asetian tradition, whose symbols, Kemetic words and basic meaning are represented at the beginning of this book.

Ka represents the vital energy that flows inside the living beings. It is the metaphysical substance that connects both spirit and matter, allowing for life to exist. Ba is something that can be more closely in parallel with the western concept of soul, the divine spark present in physical matter and having the possibility of being eternal, differing from the Ka, which can be dissipated and transmuted.

So it is the Ba that is present in every living being, at different levels of complexity and forms. Having a highly complex structure in many evolved beings, the Ba is an energy body inside which Ka circulates in its interior, going from simple systems to others as complex as the one present in the human kind and ultimately, the one present in Asetians. These last two incorporate advanced energy systems – the Shen Centers – that work like metaphysical organs, controlling and balancing the energy currents within the subtle body and are connected by a complex of *meridians*, allowing for the flux of Ka within the whole system. The meridians are, to some extent, globally aligned with the sanguine system from the physical body, being one of the main reasons why the blood is so energetically charged and has such a close relationship with vampirism.

Many times, the nature of the subtle energy is defined as being something static, predictable and having only one manifestation. To assume that is to neglect the whole dynamic nature of energy, that is composed by a whole spectrum of frequencies, with different gammas, properties and layers. The comprehension of the different types of energy is essential to the mastery of many different occult arts, any level of energy work, basic to advanced magick, natural healing techniques and, of course, vampirism.

Energy Spectrum

The whole spectrum of the subtle energy is very complex and diverse, being constituted by a large variety of frequencies. Despite that, energy is classified not only by the range of its frequency, but also by the rate and amplitude of its vibration, along with the different characteristics and manifestations from that specific type of energy.

In this book, we have compiled the most common forms of metaphysical energy, along with a short description of its characteristics and appliances in magick. These following variants of subtle energy do not represent the full spectrum, but are probably all the types you will ever need to know so you can understand and master metaphysics.

Vital Energy

Vital energy – *Ka* in Ancient Egyptian – is energy produced, assimilated or cycled by living beings with a functioning energetic system of their own. This is the main resource for vampiric feeding, a heightened type of energy within the high frequencies range, and also the reason why vampires are predators. Since Ka only exists in the living beings, the need to access it leads to the draining of this energy type from other living beings.

The Ka always has imprinted within its structure the metaphysical fingerprint of the being from where it comes from, being the reason why the vital energy from different people always has different fingerprints.

Vital energy can be charged and affected by different feelings, emotions or even thought patterns, making this a very diverse type of essence. When it is filled with these variables, it becomes denser, thicker and with higher feeding qualities. It exists in layers within the subtle system, and can range from common energy that is shared between everyone from simple interaction, to a highly intimate essence from the soul itself that can only be shared by advanced techniques of exchange or intimate interaction.

Ka is the kind of energy that flows throughout the soul and inside the subtle system of the living beings, being directly associated with their health, psyche, emotions and, of course, their powers. The higher and lower levels of Ka, although something usually not taken into consideration by humans, is of a major importance to a vampire, because it fully affects everything not only in his subtle system, as also in the physical one. These energy levels refer to the quantity and quality of the vital energy flowing within the subtle system, and can be determined by increasing the subtle sensitivity and specialized training, becoming something far more perceivable to a vampire after the awakening.

Elemental Energy

On lower and more stable energy frequencies we have the elemental energy, which refers to all the types of energy that can be drawn from the Earth, its elementals and all of the nature-related subsets.

If energy is being drained from the Moon, a thunderstorm, rain, a waterfall, the ocean or a sunset, it is elemental energy that is being absorbed by the subtle system. It usually is a fresh, very clean and pure energy, almost without any metaphysical *noise* or byproducts.

Even though this type of energy cannot be as much efficient for feeding as Ka, vampiric-wise, it can still sustain and can sure be harnessed to stabilize the energy system and spiritual empowerment. Guardians are known to master the sensing and draining of these energies, many times in an overwhelming way.

Universal Energy

The universal energy, known in the Japanese culture as *Ki*, is the rawest and purest energy form, and it can only be drawn directly from the universal source. If it is someone sending this energy for us, for example in a healing session, it can no longer be considered universal energy, since it has become vital energy because of the fact we are dealing with an energy transfusion. The energy will then carry the sender's fingerprint, along with some inherent metaphysical *noise*, like feelings, emotions and energy byproducts from its manipulation.

This is the main energy resource used in healing techniques and oriental metaphysical systems like Reiki, Tai Chi and Qi Gong. So even though this energy is very useful for healing purposes, relaxation and meditation, it cannot be used for vampiric feeding, because of the frequency, subtle structure and nature of this type of energy. Besides, if universal energy were able to sustain a vampire, any living being could be considered vampiric, since all absorb raw energy from the universe to maintain their own subtle system and energy field. This is also true because this energy type cannot be processed for vampiric powers and its frequency is insufficient for the high energy needs of a vampiric subtle metabolism.

Residual Energy

On the lowest energy frequencies spectrum we have the residual energies, which can result from a myriad of situations. Like the ambient energies generated by the passage and circulation of living beings, the stagnant energies accumulated on lesser dynamic or inactive locations, and byproducts of energy work, active manipulation, magick and even feeding.

While a vampire can slowly process this energy, it is not always a very appealing solution for feeding, not only because of the low frequency, implying a very large quantity needed to actually maintain a vampiric system, but also because of the general low quality of it. Even though in this case the variable location can be an important factor, since for example, on some religious temples, residual energy can be very heightened, due to the practices being held, as well as the dedication and Will of the participants involved in it. However, not all of the residual energies can be processed by someone's personal energy system. As a general reference, most of the ambient energies are consumable, even though of typically low quality, but energy manipulation byproducts are not assimilated or processed by vampires.

Sexual Energy

A very heightened and intimate type of energy is the one produced during sexual intercourse. The sexual energy can rapidly fill a vampire's subtle system and empower it. Basically, this type of energy is an offshoot from traditional vital energy – Ka – but because of its particularities and powerful uses, has a different nomenclature and identity of its own.

Besides vampiric feeding, sexual energy can also be used in practices of high magick, commonly known as sex magick – *Magia Sexualis* from the Latin. In these techniques, the energy generated by the sexual intercourse, arousal and orgasm, is used and directed by the Will of the practitioner to its desired intent and goal. It is also common the use of this kind of energy when working with sigils – magickal seals – that can also be empowered with techniques that rely on sexual energy.

Energy Fingerprint

Energy fingerprint is a very distinctive identification mark that every human, vampire or otherkin unconsciously and automatically leaves on all of the energy that passes through their system.

Like a signature, or a code, the energy fingerprint is what identifies everyone's personal essence and makes it unique. Also, in most of the cases, that is what makes someone's energies incompatible with your own, something that can be easily perceived under very different levels. Just like its reverse; when you feel drawn or attracted by someone's energy, it is usually because of the compatibility in his fingerprint with your own personal essence.

Amplification

The concept of amplification is highly used in the study of energy manipulation and induction. The subtle energy, commonly projected through the secondary Shen Centers located in the hands and in the eyes, sometimes needs to be amplified to a higher frequencies range, so it can be better analyzed, but especially to produce more striking results.

Minerals are one of the most common amplifiers used in energy work. Depending from its crystalline structure, constitution and conductive characteristics, different minerals react in a distinctive way to an energy beam. Likewise, each has its own specific energy field, all with different properties and behaviors. This is the reason why minerals are getting increasingly popular among natural healing treatments and meditative techniques. Even though minerals are generally used by Asetians among their practices and its metaphysical usage is a common discipline for them to master, it is out of the subject of this book to analyze and explain the properties and uses of the different types of minerals, that appear in nature in a huge variety.

Among the amplification techniques and tools, the subject that certainly causes more impact and divergent opinions is the use of a high magnification amplifier, commonly described as a *magick wand*. The use of this sort of amplifiers in magickal practices is something polemic and sometimes even made ridicule due to the proliferation of fantasy literature and cinema, which erroneously explore this old field of the high metaphysics. Talking about the active use of a wand to anyone without magickal knowledge and training invariably leads to a direct association with fiction and a high skepticism driven by the simple ignorance of the person himself. Certainly many have already been presented, in a situation or another, with a cynic smile, a doubting look, or even a more unpleasant comment, by those ignorant ones, that almost invariably share a typical evolutionary and spiritual handicap.

Magickal wands are made from solid natural materials, generally wood or a well-known mineral, and their use is called *wanding*. Its uses are diverse, from healing and meditative techniques, to an energetic weapon that can be used defensively or to deliver partial to lethal damage, and even as a powerful tool within highly advanced spiritual work. It can be used intuitively, as an analytical instrument or in scanning procedures, but can also be a proper tool in ritual work of ceremonial magick. However, the effects of a direct wand usage are not visible by the common human eye. Even to the trained energy worker the *visual effects* are always subtle, since the wand amplifies subtle energy, and nothing more, where the effects will be related with his abilities to visualize energy. The truth is, wanding easily passes unnoticed to almost everyone not related with magick, and an experienced sorcerer uses it without letting a glimpse of anything unnatural escape from its wand. For example, in a traditional wanding attack, where a counter-attack or shielding enchantment is received in response, there is nothing "magical" to be seen by the untrained eye, behind the gestures, actions and movements that the sorcerer has done when conjuring the spell.

Crystalline Amplification

The amplification of Ka through minerals, therefore having a crystalline structure, is essentially dependent from four primary factors:

- The nature of the mineral;
- The source of Ka;
- The existence of a pre-amplifier;
- The purity of the signal and its strength.

The crystallographic nature of the mineral in question, like its geological genesis, chemical composition and crystalline structure, influence the way that it affects an energy beam that trespasses it. This is going to directly affect the gammas being amplified in the energy spectrum, as well as the waves being refracted and dissipated.

On the other hand, the energy that is going to be amplified by the mineral is dependent from the initial energy source, which in the most conventional usage will be the person himself. In this case, the ability that each one has to manipulate energy, to induct stable energetic fields and homogenous Ka beams, directly affects the amplification result.

A very important issue when dealing with energy amplification through crystalline material, and many times not analyzed, is the existence, or not, of a pre-amplifier.

When passing from simple energy manipulation to a practical study of subtle energy in a non-ritualized high magick subset, it is common the use of an amplifier between the source of Ka and the amplifying mineral. To this occultist instrument we call *pre-amplifier*. This object, mediator between the source and the amplifier itself, is in many cases a magick wand, which is in fact a high vibration amplifier. The wands used in these practices are previously attuned by an *Encantatum* – an occultist adept at energy manipulation and attunement with a master degree at enchantments – with very specific techniques. In these practices, the wand is not used in a symbolic way, like in some ceremonial magick traditions, where it is used only in a ritualistic context. Here it is an active component in a process of energy manipulation. That is why the term *active magick* is used when referring to this sort of techniques.

In the case of the signal being previously amplified by a wand, the beam that will be projected by the mineral will have a different intensity and frequency from a situation without the existence of a pre-amplifier, like in the practice of Reiki, where the energy is induced directly from the secondary Shen Centers of the practitioner, as the ones located in the hands and in the eyes.

Then we have the purity of the signal and its strength as conditioning factors of crystalline amplification. These variables are very closely connected with the second factor previously described – the source of the energy field. The more pure the signal being transmitted, the more predictable and analytical results are achieved, because most of the known Ka spectrum is present in the projected beam. On the other hand, if the energy beam transmitted is impure and with a lot of metaphysical noise, the amplification will certainly be affected by these alterations in the energy field. These impurities in the energy being projected can go from something as subtle as underlying errors in the transmission, to more complex variables like religious dogmas and feelings transmitted and crystallized in the projected energy, consciously or not.

Incense

The use of burning incense can be quite beneficial in the mastery of energy work. The inhalation of the smoke produced by the incense will alter the individual when being absorbed into his system, flowing through the blood stream, slowing the airflow and heartbeat. In this way, the incense is a tool in helping to achieve altered states of consciousness, being a conditioning factor in the process of manipulating energy, especially when some sort of meditation and concentration is needed to gain focus.

The usage of incense does not only have physical effects, but metaphysical ones as well. An ambient with flowing incense is more easily charged by energy. Since this type of smoke works as a conductor of energy, when it fills the space of a room, the air gets thicker and naturally conductive, so the energy is more easily transmitted and projected. This is a small detail in why a lethal charge of energy dumped directly in the Heart Shen is far more effective when projected in a smoky incense environment.

Also to note that all of this is valid when using high quality incense, hand rolled, preferably from India or handmade by someone trustworthy, versed in the art of crafting incense. Bad quality incense, with unnatural products, might change the desired effect of its use. So always keep that in mind when adding incense burning to your magickal practices.

Subtle Anatomy

The study of the energy body and all of the partial structures that constitute it, like the Shen Centers and the meridians, to the outer shells that protects it and interacts with the two worlds, the physical and the energetic, is called subtle anatomy.

Different beings have different subtle bodies, resulting in a diverse anatomy for a myriad of species. Irrational animals also have an energy body in parallel with their physical one, commonly with very few Shen Centers and a more simple system of meridians, but their subtle anatomy is out of the subject of this book. We are going to dwell in the particularities of the subtle bodies from vampires, especially Asetians, which draw many similarities with the energy systems found in humans and other evolved otherkin, although having some more advanced *features* and structures.

With this in mind, some restrictive characteristics do apply, like the existence of tendril networks on the outer layers of the subtle body, which will be described more in detail along the next few chapters. So every time a reference will be done to a subtle body, a Shen system, or anything related with general subtle anatomy, it will be assuming an Asetian subtle anatomy analysis and referring to vampiric energy systems, if not mentioned otherwise.

Subtle anatomy is an occult science in its own right, having many concepts with its roots in times long gone, but which modern and scientific development has obtained additional knowledge in recent occultist studies and research. Like other information, the validation of these concepts and theories have been analyzed and confirmed under experimental processes and extensive studies. But since development and new conclusions are achieved daily, some details are subject of change in the future, just like in the physical anatomy and traditional medicine where, even more than in the occult sciences, theories and concepts are changed on a common and regular basis.

Aura and Tendrils

The subtle body, along with all its complexity of organs and energy-conductive filaments, is protected inside an outer shell formed from dense and flexible energy. This energy system is called aura.

The aura has a layered structure, with increasing density of energy in the direction of the subtle body. The outer layers are very thin and the energy that forms them is a lot more disperse than in the inner ones. This happens because of a natural process of slow energy release and cycling. Since the subtle body is continuously absorbing raw energy from the source and impure energy from the environment, these energies work like filling a glass of water. If you continuously let the water run inside it, this water will get mixed inside the contents of the glass and some of these contents will spill out from the glass once it is full, being released into the environment. That is what happens with the subtle body, the absorbed energies will flow into the system, and some of the energies kept on the inside will slowly be flushed out. This process is done through the aura system, being one of the reasons why it is constituted by layers of energy. These layers will slowly get detached from the aura, so the thin outer ones get lost and dispersed into the surrounding environment, and the subtle body processes another thick energy layer into the inner frame of the aura.

The vampiric aura has a very specific condition among its structure, which helps in the interaction with outside energy, active manipulation and in the overall process of feeding. The energy layers are populated by very small and thin subtle filaments, constituted by highly elastic energy, allowing for them to stretch up to considerable distances. These energy filaments are called *tendrils*. Besides being elastic, the nature of the energy that forms these tiny structures allows for them to be easily molded and manipulated according to the vampire's Will, resulting in very effective energy tools from defensive to offensive situations.

Being the outer shell of the subtle body, the aura represents the energy that others usually have the chance to *taste* and feel from yourself. So it represents a very important factor of what others perceive from you and the first opinions and impressions that your presence causes on others and in the environment. In this way, the change of the form and feel of the aura is a very valuable tool for vampires, since it can be used to influence others and allow them to perceive what you want them to know and feel about yourself. These techniques of vampiric manipulation known as *Projecting* are something that Asetians are adept at, and commonly use on a daily basis, many times even unconsciously. So, the ability to shape and shift the aura is usually seen as something purely vampiric, and even though it sure is a common *power* among Asetians, it can also be achieved by a human who is an advanced energy practitioner, but not at the extent and ease that vampires do. This is true mainly because when a vampire changes his aura, it does not only affect the layers from it, but also shape it with the aid of the tendrils that can easily change their appearance and form. So humans, as not having tendrils within their subtle structure, can never achieve the same results of aura shifting as Asetians do.

Subtle Body

The whole energy-composed structure that exists inside the aura is the subtle body, also called energy body or astral body. This is the structure that sustains the Shen Centers and the meridians, unifying the whole complexity of the various energy systems. In the Asetian tradition, the subtle body is many times referred to as Ba – Ancient Egyptian word for soul – and it is the energy structure closer to the western definition of spirit and soul.

This metaphysical psycho-spiritual body is formed by a type of energy that does not dissipate or fade away. It can be wounded and destroyed, but also has the ability to become eternal, being that not a birthright, but a conquerable condition. This is the main structure responsible for the vampiric immortality. In the case of the Asetians, the soul and whole essence is different from humans, not only being immortal, but also divine.

The health of the Ba is of fundamental importance to every living being, since the state of the subtle body constantly echoes to the physical realm, manifesting in the condition of the physical body. The vast majority of physical conditions, diseases and unbalances have a subtle cause at its genesis. So keeping the balance of the subtle body and a healthy flow of its internal energies and systems is a very important factor for a balanced and healthy mind and body.

Meridians

Between the various energy organs, many filaments of energy exist to transport vital energy inside the subtle body. These energy-conductive filaments are called *meridians*. This name has its origins in the Chinese *jing-luo* and it is a widely used concept in Traditional Chinese Medicine, being also found in different cultures with a well-established knowledge of the subtle energy systems, like the word *Nadis* in the Hindu system, with its roots from the Sanskrit *Nad* and meaning channel.

At some extent, the meridians are globally aligned with the physical body's sanguine system, working in a way that resembles the blood vessels. They vary in size and diameter; while some are larger and thicker, allowing for a higher flow of energy, others are thinner and more fragile, like the veins and arteries in the physical blood system.

The meridians play an important role in oriental treatments like acupuncture and acupressure, where blockages in the flow of the energy inside the meridians are broken, or the flow in the stream is inverted, by the use of needles, energy and pressure. These specific points in the meridians are called *acupoints* in Traditional Chinese Medicine and *tsubo* in the Japanese practices. However, some acupoints might not be located on the meridians, but in small groups forming microsystems of acupoints, located for example in secondary and tertiary Shen. The majority of the acupoints are considered a tertiary Shen on a subtle anatomy basis.

Shen Centers

The subtle body has in its internal structure a few complex systems that work in part like energy organs, controlling and balancing the flux of Ka through the whole system. These structures are called by the Asetians as *Shen*, and are considered nexus of vital energy, commonly known out of the Kemetic world by the name *Chakra*. The word Shen is Kemetic and means ring or circle, being also a symbol of eternity, because it has no beginning and no end. Its hieroglyph is similar to a royal cartouche, which can contain divine names, pharaohs or composed sigils, but has a circular form and no contents inside the ring. It is a solar symbol, that can be seen in the representation of the Crown Shen of several deities, many times wrongly identified as a representation of the Sun, when in fact symbolizes an inner feature – an energy center – that by its high concentration of energy was symbolized by a solar disk. This is something that can be found repeatedly in the symbolism and art from Kemet.

The energy structure itself has a circular diffuse form and rotates. The rotation direction and speed is dependant from the health and functioning of the Shen itself. It is possible to have no movement at all, in cases of highly stagnant and polluted energies, resulting in fully blocked Shen centers, where immediate energy care and treatment should be considered.

While much of this knowledge was already known by the ancient Egyptians, other information dues to more recent studies and development both under occult sciences and holistic medicine. Some concepts being currently used have parallels in the Asian metaphysical knowledge and Hinduism practices, having the word Chakra a genesis on the Sanskrit *Cakra*, meaning wheel and circle. However, the whole concept behind the metaphysical system of Chakras is far older, having its roots in the Asetian system of Shen Centers, as is represented for example in the overall architecture of the Temple of Luxor located in the ancient city of Thebes in Egypt, and dates all the way back to the teachings of the Sep Tepy.[7]

There are three distinctive types of Shen systems: the primary, the secondary and the tertiary. The primary energy centers are seven, being aligned with the major endocrine glands in the physical body and with the central backbone of the skeleton, each of the center correlating to major nerve ganglia branching forth from the spinal column. These organs are interconnected by the meridians, which allow for the flow of Ka between the different Shen and the rest of the subtle body, being fundamental structures of the whole energy system.

On a more complex approach, the Shen also correlate with levels of consciousness, metaphysical manifestations, emotional states, physical conditions, archetypical figures, colors, sounds, tastes and many other variables...

In this way, Shen Centers are very important structures in a myriad of spiritual and metaphysical practices like energy work, psychic attack and defense, healing, balancing, meditating and more advanced techniques like subtle surgery. Its study and solid understanding is crucial in these techniques, to the mastery of different occult sciences, and to the personal evolution itself.

Individual Shen Systems

In the following pages will be described the different characteristics and associations of the seven main Shen Centers. The systems composing the secondary and tertiary Shen will not be described, since they form an extensive and complex subtle system that is out of this book's desired approach, and can be better consulted in Asetian specific texts on subtle anatomy and works on holistic healing techniques.

For a better use of these concepts and information in a more medical and practical situation, we have condensed and categorized most of the information in a table layout for a fast and easy access, working as a reference on Shen characteristics. These tables can be found on this book's Appendices, under the Shen System Tables subset.

Root Shen

The Root Shen is the first of the seven main Shen Centers and it is the one that is located lower on the physical system. In the Asetian system it is represented by the *Was* Sacred Pillar.

Physically, it is located in the perineum. Associated with the colors red and black, this Shen is closely connected to the element Earth. The related functions are vitality, strength, survival and instincts. Some minerals that more closely resonate with this specific Shen are the ruby, red jasper, obsidian, black tourmaline and hematite – a stone intimately related with blood.

This Shen affects primarily the spinal column, the anus and the rectum, the colon and most of the legs extension.

If balanced, it can enhance the physical body, strengthen the connection with the material world, increasing grounding, stability and promoting courage. When unbalanced it promotes violence, anger, tension and a self-centered behavioral pattern.

Sexual Shen

The Sexual Shen is the second in the system and it is intimately related with the libidinous system – physically and mentally. It is connected with the *Tiet* Sacred Pillar in the Asetian culture.

The Shen is located in the lower abdomen, on top of the bladder. Orange is the related color, even though being a Shen connected with the element Water. It controls functions of sexuality, vitality and intense energy. The carnelian and the amber – not a true mineral, being organic and amorphous – are in close vibration with this Shen.

The function of the Sexual Shen affects mainly the bladder, genitals, ovaries, testicles, kidneys and the suprarenal glands.

When healthy, it balances emotions, desire, pleasure, sexuality, promotes movement and allows surrender. But if unbalanced, it results in sexual problems, confusion, and feelings of jealousy, envy and possession.

Solar Plexus Shen

The third of the main Shen Centers is the Solar Plexus, having the *Ba* as the Asetian Sacred Pillar related with this energy organ.

The Shen is located below the chest, and it is related with the color yellow of the bright Sun, being Fire the associated element. It controls functions in the nervous and digestive systems, balances the whole system's metabolism, both physically and energetically and interferes with emotions. Common stones used in this Shen are the citrine and tiger's eye.

Physically, this Shen affects the stomach, liver, nervous system and the pancreas.

When balanced, the Solar Plexus enhances Will and authority, promotes energy flow through the whole system and increases self-control, unleashing transformation. But if unregulated, it can create anger, fear, paranoia, depression, hate and manifest physically by digestive problems.

Heart Shen

The fourth energy centre of the system is the Heart Shen, with a close connection to blood. Inside the Asetian subtle system it connects with the *Ib* Sacred Pillar.

Its location is in the center of the chest, above the sternum. It can be related with green and rose colors, and it is associated with the element of Air. It has functions associated with blood, life force and circulation. Being the emerald, green tourmaline, green jade and rose quartz the minerals associated with this Shen.

This energy center controls the function of the heart, circulatory system, the lungs and even the arms and hands.

If healthy, this Shen will promote forgiveness, compassion, understanding and acceptance, enhance feelings of peace and open the Self to true love. But if working out of balance, might induce repression of feelings, general unbalance, and echo to the physical realm by heart and lung problems.

Throat Shen

The Shen of the Throat is the fifth in the energy system. It is connected with the *Khepri* Sacred Pillar from the Asetian mysteries.

Physically it is located at the center of the throat, and the associated color is blue. The element for this Shen is sound and vibration. It affects the speech, sound, vibration, communication abilities and creativity. It connects with the energies from the turquoise and lapis lazuli stones.

The functioning of this energy center affects the thyroid, throat, mouth and teeth.

When balanced promotes control over the spoken word and effective communication, but if unhealthy causes problems in the speech and general communication, or manifests in the form of ignorance.

Third Eye Shen

One of the most important Shen Centers in the magickal practices is the Third Eye. It is the number six in the main Shen global structure and to the Asetians it is connected with the *Ka* Sacred Pillar.

It is located in the center of the forehead, between the eyebrows and the associated color is indigo or dark blue. On a more elemental level, it is related with the psychic powers, and correlates with activities like psychic projection, energy manipulation, vision and general brain functions. Lapis lazuli and sodalite are both stones that connect with these energy vibrations.

The Third Eye is connected with the eyes, nose and ears, affecting their health and functions.

If working healthy, this Shen enhances intuition, insight, imagination, clairvoyance and Will, opening doors to realization of the soul. When unbalanced, it manifests by lack of concentration, lower metaphysical sensitivity, headaches, tension, eye problems and bad dreams.

Crown Shen

The last of the main Shen Centers is the Crown, being the number seven, and the one that expands more beyond the physical body. In the Asetian system it is related with the *Ankh* Sacred Pillar, a connection with the infinite.

It is located on the top of the head, expanding upwards, and the color is Violet, with an intimate relation with the divine connection from the Asetians to the Violet Flame of Isis. The ruling element is the Spirit and the Divine. This Shen works mainly as a connection with the Divinity and as a source of raw universal energy. The minerals that vibrate with these energies are the amethyst, diamond and fluorite.

The Crown Shen physically interferes mainly with the function of the brain.

When this Shen is balanced, it promotes the unification with the Higher Self and the Divine, sense of oneness and perception of the infinite reality. But if allowed to get unbalanced, it manifests by confusion, depression, lack of spirituality and senility.

Shen Anatomy

On this page can be found a map of the Shen anatomy in the Asetian system, which can also be consulted as a larger version in the Appendices. In this map there are represented the seven main Shen Centers on the left column and the seven secondary ones on the right. The tertiary Shen Centers are not represented in this map because of the high number in which they are found in the subtle body, being diverse and also hard to locate on such a general description of physical location. Many of the tertiary Shen are acupoints, extensively used and described in the works of Acupuncture and Traditional Chinese Medicine.

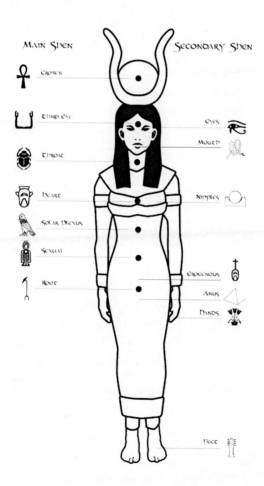

Wounds

The subtle body can be injured. The underlying causes of these wounds can be many, from simple and mundane situations, like depression, to more metaphysical situations like energy attacks.

The wounds are mainly located in the layers of the aura, with the deepness depending on the intensity of the attack. This kind of wounds, while superficial, will take some amount of time to heal. The healing process will be assured by the core energy system, and the wound will slowly disappear as new inner layers are produced by the subtle body into the aura and the outer ones get dumped into the environment. The process can be accelerated by energy healing techniques, which will also strengthen the aura itself.

Other types of wounds, more problematic and internal, are the ones that manifest in the subtle body itself, or in any energy center like a Shen. These wounds are usually the result of advanced energy attacks, intense torture – physical or energetical – or deep trauma, like a severe accident or death. This kind of wounds are deep and dangerous, requiring a large amount of time to heal, sometimes even lifetimes. In the severest cases, the subtle body will need your active metaphysical assistance in the healing process, or from a therapist knowledgeable in energy healing and subtle anatomy, while the energy body slowly refills the wounded zone with fresh and clean energy.

The most complex and deep wounds in the energy body can prevent a soul from reincarnating for long periods of time, since the aura needs a minimum healthy state to pass through the incarnation process. Otherwise it is obliged to stay in the in-between lives realm, slowly recovering. Because of this, energy torture techniques and intense psychic attacks were praised metaphysical weapons in the old days, used both by vampires and against them. In the metaphysical Epic Wars, most of them now long gone, energy played a central and crucial variable to both defensive and offensive actions, being still a widely studied subject nowadays inside the occult orders like the Aset Ka.

Blockages

One of the most common health problems in the energy system is the development of blockages. They are mostly concentrations of energy that get more solid and fix to a place in the subtle system. Usually, the main cause of the development of blockages is energy stagnation. Many factors can lead to stagnation, and when this develops on a specific location in the subtle body, if allowed to solidify, it will transform into an energy blockage.

The better method to cure metaphysical blockages is energy healing. A direct beam of energy with a steady frequency and vibration into the area of the blockage helps to dissolve this energy and promotes energy flow inside the system. However, not always this procedure is strong enough to break the blockage and dissolve it, so sometimes more intense energy techniques are necessary if a cure is to be achieved. It is important to keep in mind that the best course of action is prevention. A healthy diet, meditation and energy practice are the most efficient ways to achieve a healthy and balanced energy system, keeping a holistic thought in mind, to a well connected mind, body and spirit.

Blockages and energy stagnation echo to the physical and psychological realm in the form of disease, being the main causes of nineteen percent of all ailments.

Tumors

If an energy blockage is allowed to encrust and develop for a long period of time it can become an energy tumor. These tumors echo to the physical realm in a very negative and malignant way, manifesting in complicated health issues and even cancers.

To this kind of malignant encrusted energies, treatments with simple energy beams will not be effective, although it can allow an ease of the symptoms, prevention of proliferation and pain control. In these cases, more advanced and intense methods of energy healing and holistic treatment is demanded, and the recovery will be slow and sometimes complicated.

If a tumor is allowed to endure, it can manifest after death in weakened energy bodies and other problems.

Links

Links are energy tunnels that are built spontaneously on more close and intimate interactions between living beings, or intentionally crafted by the means of ritual and magick. During sexual intercourse, romantic interactions, intimate friendships or deep feeds, the energy system forges a subtle link with the other person. A link does not need physical contact to be created; it can simply rely on emotion, becoming the actual invisible tunnel that sustains those feelings.

There are simple and tiny links that easily dissipate with time and others stronger and thicker that, despite being very hard to break, can linger until death, or in some more special cases, remain undestroyed through lifetimes. The special and eternal bonds that exist between some of the Asetians are this kind of strong and unbreakable links.

Every time you interact with someone with whom you have forged an energy link, the link will be strengthened, especially in emotional situations, both good and bad. This is a very important reason why vampires should be very cautious about from whom they feed. While a direct contact drain will leave only a thin link that will dissipate very soon, scaring only the aura of the donor, a deep feed will create a very strong link, that in some cases can puncture through the aura and into the soul, accessing the very core of the energy system.

Links can be used actively if enough sensitivity is developed. Since energy can be sent through them to the other end, they can be used to send feelings and emotions, as to draw and send energy. This connection can become apparent in situations of empathy between two beings, when people sometimes *feel* the emotional state of the other or when the other is in grave danger and needs help. However, while links can also be used to transfer thoughts and information, actually being the mechanism behind the way that silent communication and telepathy works, they are not fully reliable, since subtle links are easily affected by metaphysical noise and the energy can be lost through dissipation during its travel, resulting in not very accurate practices.

Furthermore, energy links are something to be very careful about, since they can work as a security leak into your subtle system. Even the weakest links are directly connected to the aura, which means that they have free access through your external energy shields.

Links can be severed and cauterized, but only if any interaction with the owner of the other end is completely stopped, or that would reconnect the link and reinforce its connection. Even the treatment to destroy this kind of connections is to be avoided, since it harasses the energy body and leaves an open wound in the aura, which again can be exploited by malignant entities. When dealing with these situations, energy shielding techniques should be mastered and protective precautions should be taken into consideration at all times. If the decision is made to actively remove the energy link, the procedure should only be done by an experienced practitioner in the arts of subtle surgery.

ENERGY WORK

A long this chapter are going to be summarized the basic concepts needed in the practices of energy work, defining a framework that can sustain higher spiritual practices and vampirical metaphysics. The concepts approached in here are regular practices in the Asetian tradition, and represent a background needed in more advanced techniques discussed on the next chapters. Gaining mastery over these subjects is of considerable importance, allowing for getting into other more advanced subjects in metaphysics with success and efficiency.

Certainly most of the concepts described in this chapter represent something very easy to understand, that many will eventually know from practice and even master it for a long time. While some might already have had metaphysical training in this sort of magickal work, and others might have always known how to do it as an inborn ability, this information is still relevant as a reference and source to different concepts of energy work, and the mechanisms behind what you are really doing in every specific situation of magickal approach.

Meditation

One of the most intrinsic practices to achieve a controlled and efficient energy work is to know how to consciously meditate. The achievement of meditative states and trances are a common practice among Asetians, which rely on these techniques as steps into other realities and to accomplish metaphysical work.

Meditation proves to be a valuable tool to relaxation and self-therapy, helping in the process of rebalancing the mind, the body and the spirit. The equilibrium of the subtle body is a very delicate state, and hard to achieve, for a vampire. Because of this, the practice of meditation on a regular basis is one of the first steps to anyone starting into the realms of magick. Despite the balancing factor, meditation is also an obvious mechanism of energy recovery, which like sleeping, can enhance a vampire in a weakened energy state.

Grounding

Grounding can be a complementary technique to meditation, a basic pre-requisite to energy work and a useful tool to anyone that has a great connection with energy, like vampires. It allows the strengthening of your subtle body's connection with the Earth, allowing for the excess of energy and metaphysical byproducts to be plunged as well with detrimental energy to your own system. This proves to be a good method to achieve balance and get some focus. To anyone with a constant interaction with energy, like Asetians, being in crowded places can become a problem. The different kinds of energies, vibrations and thoughts floating around can become overwhelming, manifesting through dizziness, confusion, headache and other sensations, that can be balanced by grounding and shielding techniques. The constant mixed thoughts in a congested environment can be very detrimental to the mind and energy of a vampire, who would easily capture and interpret these external signals because of his native empathy with the subtle realm. All of these situations can benefit from grounding techniques and make use of it to find the desired equilibrium.

Guardians are exceptionally gifted in the arts of grounding and dumping energies, which despite being a great defensive asset that propitiates a more effective channeling of the malignant energies from a harmful spell that was cast at them, can also be used on everyday practice, to get rid of unwanted energies and strengthening of their subtle shields. In ritual and non solitary energy work, the Guardians are a true obelisk, ensuring a safe practice not only defensively but also allowing the disposal of byproducts from the metaphysical work, that otherwise would unhealthily remain on the system of the participants. Viperines and Concubines tend to strongly benefit from the presence and working of a Guardian, which can rebalance their highly chaotic system and ensure a more effective release of accumulated energies generated by the permanent energy flow from these lineages. A Guardian also propitiates them balance and strength through their potent inner shields.

The grounding from the Guardian lineage is so effective, that they have been seen dumping a massive amount of energy nearly without effort. Asetians from this lineage are so used to do it unconsciously, that an issue might be to do it consciously and under control, but being something that can be easily sorted with just a little training.

An effective grounding relies on a strong connection to the Earth, usually done through the Root Shen or the lower secondary Shen Centers, using it as an outlet for the dumped energies. It is important for this connecting to be both solid and stable, otherwise the unwanted energies might not be efficiently plunged. While a very practical procedure, grounding can also induce a heightened connection with the Earth, dumping disproportionate quantities of energy and leading to a point of excessive grounding. This is not an advisable situation to any vampire, since he is a being that relies on his energy interaction to keep a stable system, where an immoderate grounding can lead to a lack of sensitivity towards energy. These situations can be corrected using a technique opposed to grounding, inverting its process and allowing achieving a more balanced state. These techniques, known as *Mirror Grounding* or *Inverted Grounding*, rely on establishing a link towards the Air, and using this connection to rebalance the energy state and overall dumping procedures of the internal system, finding a stable balance.

Due to the subtle characteristics of the grounding procedures, they are commonly used prior to many practices of energy work, together with a complementary technique called *centering*.

Centering

The practice of centering is a common procedure in energy work, usually done after grounding and complementing it. Actually, both techniques complement each other so directly that many people use it indifferently, like a single procedure, enhancing the overall practice.

Centering is literally locating your own center and aligning it. The core of the subtle body is located differently in everyone, and easily changes and gets misaligned due to many problems, both physical and mental, and sometimes derived from such simple things as stress. The correction of this alignment problem in the subtle center is crucial, not only to achieve a healthy energy body, but simply to anyone dealing with energy. This is true since only its stability, correct functioning and coordination with the rest of the system can assure a proper work in metaphysics and magick.

The process of centering includes locating this energy kernel deep inside you, energizing it and making it rotate, and then aligning it. It is also common to be proceeded by an expansion of the gathered energy in your center, impregnated with your fingerprint, to the limits of your subtle body, rebalancing it. If grounding was done previously to the centering technique, the system is already cleansed and rid of energy byproducts and vibrations extraneous to your subtle body. In this way being ready to an overall rebalance of the system and rehash of the kernel, helping it to work effectively, sane and stable.

Sensing

Manipulating energy is an inborn ability common to all Asetians. However, not everyone is totally aware of his constant interaction with the subtle realm, in this way not always being sensitive to energy, being a major reason of concern to any vampire, which highly depends on his interaction with energy. This is something that can be easily fixed by learning the Asetian ways, increasing exponentially their own sensitivity and abilities during the process of awakening. Viperines are the ones with a greater sensitivity towards energy work and awareness of the subtle realm, commonly dealing and interacting with it unconsciously all their lives and manipulating it prior to awakening. The other two lineages usually aren't this sensitive, but can also learn to master it, with time, dedication and proper training. A few already do it consciously prior to awakening as well.

When it comes to sensing and manipulating energy, the hands are great metaphysical tools. The highly developed secondary Shen Centers located in the hands of the Asetians, can be seen represented in the Asetian Shen Map presented on the chapter on *Subtle Anatomy*. The mastery of the ability to channel and project energy through these specific outlets is a major asset in energy work, especially when it comes to intentional and direct projection of Ka. Because of this, the hands and the eyes are commonly seen as weapons to the vampire, who can use them effectively in an offensive way, due to the easiness of energy projection through this kind of Shen Centers.

Energy can be sensed in different ways, depending on the individual, and there is no way better than another. Some people easily feel it, while others have more easiness in seeing it. All ways are valid, as long as it works for that specific person. Although energy sensing is not a main condition in being able to manipulate it, it sure can propitiate a more effective work and especially a more controlled and conscious craft, than someone manipulating it without being able to sense it, even though possible. The sensing of the energy enhances awareness of the subtle reality, making it easier to consciously direct and shape it.

Breath and Look

The use of the breath and the look to direct energy is a common practice in metaphysics, being acceptable tools to the focus of Will. While directing energy can be independent from the breath and look, it is commonly affected by it. A controlled breathing can help in stabilizing the flow of the energy being projected or manipulated, with the controlled and desired vibration. It is also a very useful way to concentrate and aid visualization.

The mind is the greater energy shaper of all. Dreams, thoughts and emotions are all built from energy. In this way, it is easy to understand that thinking is molding energy around us, projecting and absorbing it. That is why active visualization is such a regular technique within energy work, since with the proper tools and techniques, visualizing can truly be manipulating the energy and achieving what is being seen in the mind's eye.

Despite the breath and look being great centers of focus to gather our Will, that is not the only reason why they are so widely used in the direction and guiding of energy by vampires. They also represent two important secondary Shen, which have an internal structure specially designed and adapted to this sort of metaphysical procedure. Like the major energy centers – the primary Shen – the secondary ones have a specific structure, internal anatomy and functioning, interacting differently with energy and working in distinctive ways, being used in magick and metaphysics under differential applications and practices.

Cleansing

Metaphysical cleansing is a group of techniques categorized under the energy work practices, used on a regular basis by the Asetians. These techniques ensure the energetic cleaning of any specific object, location or individual, and can include a physical purification bath, but always include a subtle one with a flow of pure, clean energy.

Cleansing is done prior to any attunement or energization ritual done to an amulet, talisman, wand or other magickal instrument. It allows the object to get rid of stagnant energy, impurities and vibrations that are alien to its nature, getting it ready for the energizing procedure itself.

There are many techniques used to energetically cleanse. The more personal ways for the Asetians rely on the use of the Violet Flame, that is an energy vibration exclusive to the Asetian usage, although this sort of high vibrations is even more commonly used to magickal attunements and syntonization techniques.

Healing

As was described in the chapter about the Asetian tradition, the bloodline of Aset has inborn healing abilities like their divine mother. The exceptional skills that the Asetians possess to manipulate and interact with energy leaves them with a great potential towards natural healing and traditional medicine currents. Even their vampiric qualities, that enhances their predatory weapons, allowing the draining of life force from others, can prove to be very efficient healing tools in cases of stagnated energy, blockages and energy tumors, but can also be detrimental to the vampire practitioner if used without caution. However, this does not mean that all vampires are healers. Although they have this innate quality, many do not dedicate their skills towards this mundane pursuit, but more to self-development achievements, towards enlightenment, in the quest for their lost alchemy of the soul.

Despite the myriad of natural healing techniques and available knowledge from the traditional medicine variants, the Asetians also possess another healing instrument, a lot less known but sometimes far more effective – Kemetic Medicine. Part of this sacred knowledge has been kept secret inside the Order of Aset Ka for thousands of years, usually only practiced by the Temple priests and Asetian physicians, and many of these teachings have been lost throughout time, in the wars and conflicts that history has put in our ways.

Energy healing is certainly one of the most well mastered subjects inside the natural therapies spectrum for an Asetian practitioner. This type of vibrational medicine is very useful for vampires, who are more aware of their subtle maladies and have energy systems that more easily echo into the physical realm, manifesting their energetic instabilities and subtle unbalances in the form of diseases, depression and psychological problems. That is why vampires are known to practice self-healing, meditation and energization techniques, in order to regain their inner balance, stabilize their energy system and promote a healthy flow. A being that constantly interacts with energy, molding, manipulating and projecting it, easily gets byproducts of this energy work stuck inside his own subtle body, developing blockages, malignant attachments, undesired energy links and other problems that unbalance his system and collapses his health, needing treatment by specialized metaphysical care.

Cycling

The process of cycling is an energy practice that circulates vital energy throughout the subtle system, without consuming but processing it, heightening its state and increasing its overall quality and vibration. This is a technique that, although globally practiced by all lineages, is particularly inborn to Concubines, who do it constantly, leading to some of their problems like instability, confusion and mental issues.

Cycling not only works as an effective technique to refine and intensify energy, but also as reliable way to promote energy flow and fight stagnation. In this way, it is a valuable procedure to Guardians, that with their strong powerful energies and shields are not used to the practice of cycling, and can even become overwhelmed by the chaotic nature of the cycling and the sensations promoted by it. These energy obelisks, that the natives from the Guardian lineage truly are, can be very helpful to people with an uncontrolled cycling, like Concubines, helping in their stabilization and rebalance.

Cycling can be used not only internally, as described, but also externally, to increase the quality of the energy found in a specific physical location. During this process, the energy is absorbed from the environment, cycled through the system and intensified, and then released back into the physical realm. This allows for the intensification of the energy from a specific place, or to charge it with a special emotion, feel or vibration. The energy inside the Asetian Temples is usually highly cleansed and intensified with these techniques, but it is also common for the Asetians to apply this knowledge in their ritual chambers or their private havens, like their sleeping rooms.

The cycling techniques not only promote a healthy flow of energy while intensifying it and increasing its quality, but also condense the energy, making it thicker and denser, and more effective in ritual and magick. Vampires are well aware that a small amount of high-quality energy is far more sustaining than a big amount of poor-quality essence, being a direct reason why donors care with so much caution for their subtle energies and sacred essence, keeping a healthy flow of energy and a dense and heightened state to their inner vibrations. Asetians are known to maximize their feedings if practiced inside their bloodline and metaphysical family, being the better way to optimize the procedure to both vampire and donor. It is easy to understand how highly important is the caring and maintenance of their own inner energy, not only to balance and health, but also because it is common to some Asetians to live both as vampires and donors, inside their sacred metaphysical family.

VAMPIRIC MANIPULATION

Vampiric manipulation deals with energy work and metaphysics specific to vampires. While a few of the forth-mentioned concepts can be learnt by some skilled humans, its efficiency is hardly even near the vampiric practice, that relies on the inborn abilities and metaphysically-ready subtle system from the otherkin. Because of this, vampires should always be approached with caution, when it comes to magick and direct energy manipulation. With the sensitive vampiric system, not only can energy attacks and scans be more easily sensed and detected, but also can be expected metaphysical attacks and defensive mechanisms far more effective than from regular energy workers in the human kind.

Most of the practices included in this chapter are of important interest to vampires, because of its direct application in everyday life. Most of the concepts are not very relevant for humans, with the exception of shielding, that can be useful when looking for defensive techniques against magickal attacks and how to deal with an unknown vampire.

Shielding

Shielding is one of the most mentioned techniques when dealing with active energy work, and it is the most important discipline in defensive magick. Everyone has inborn natural energy shields, although they are typically thin and ineffective to an intentional attack, being the reason why an important discipline of energy-shield development and mastery was developed ever since the times when magick was being used. Humans are not usually aware of their subtle shields, and deal with them unconsciously, commonly having no control over its working and not being able to manipulate them effectively. On the other hand, vampires have full control over their shields, and with proper training they can easily mutate them at their own will.

There are two main types of metaphysical shields: the primary ones and secondary ones. The primary shield is a natural energy field that surrounds every living being, a coating of defensive energy floating right above the outer layers of the aura. These shields are inborn to everyone, and constitute the last line of defense of the subtle body. If undeveloped they are usually thin, and permeable, being stronger in some individuals and weaker in others. Asetians from the Guardian lineage have especially strong and developed inborn energy shields, and have a special talent to manipulate and enforce them. Because of this, they have very powerful defense mechanisms, being one of the hardest incarnated beings to magickally attack.

Secondary shields are unnatural forces created by magickal abilities from the practitioner, using techniques of energy work to create an artificial defense barrier above the primary energy shield. These shields can be very potent and strong, and are usually bound to an amulet or talisman, amplifying mineral or magick wand. The secondary energy shields are fueled by vital force, so they must be used with caution and under conscious control, since they can easily drain out the subtle system, highly dropping its energy levels. Guardians do not need as frequently to rely on secondary shields, since the density of their primary ones can usually be parallel with the sum of the primary and secondary shields of an average vampire, making the need of an additional energy shield useless in many cases. This is true not only in general practice, but even in magickal confrontations on the field. However, some Guardians might find useful the binding to an amulet of a secondary shield of a special vibration, to accomplish a certain goal with a concrete objective in mind, like it is commonly used by the other two lineages. It is important to keep in mind that secondary shields will deteriorate over time, since they are made out of manipulated vital energy, which although condensed, will slowly dissipate. Acknowledging this, the energy level of the shield should be kept under surveillance, and its integrity and balance enforced periodically, so it does not collapse if it is still needed.

This kind of shields are very useful in crowded environments, where the flood of many people's energy and the mixing of these vibrations can have a negative impact on the vampire's energy system and affect his inner balance. The effects of this energy pollution can manifest from simple headaches, dizziness and confusion to more instable conditions if the subtle system reaches a point of collapse. Especially for the highly sensitive lineages, like the Viperines, the use of energy shields when in contact with different people and in public places might be of a great value. However, the excessive use of shields might also be a problem, since while they block undesired energies from reaching the subtle body, they are an effective subtle barrier, that prevents most of the energy exchanges with the environment, and by this lowering the energy sensitivity and subtle awareness, that are of major importance to any vampire, but especially to Viperines that rely on this great connection with the etheric to maintain stability.

Although shields are more widely seen as the defensive energy barriers described above, shielding is also commonly used in the practice of spells and enchantments, even though many times the practitioner is not really aware that what is being created is simply an energy shield. For example in the case of an offensive spell being conjured, or a direct psychic attack, the sorcerer sometimes rely on counter-spells to diverge the malignant spell's energy. These counter-spells and defensive enchantments, despite being more complex than regular energy shields, constitute in fact just an offshoot of an advanced secondary shield, being applied in a specific point in time and fueled by a high stream of energy, reason why they are not permanent.

Projecting

The ability to *project* is a renowned characteristic of the vampire, particularly developed in the Viperine lineage. *Projecting* is a metaphysical mechanism, and technique, that relies in the release and directional projection of energy with a specific vibration, charged with a particular emotion and feel. This procedure can be done consciously, in situations like social manipulation, but it is also done unconsciously on a regular basis by the Asetian bloodline.

The mechanism known as projecting is a powerful tool and a fearful weapon that in many kinds of manipulation, when properly mastered, is highly effective and potentially dangerous. It allows for the vampire to pass an image of himself, designed at his taste and adapted to the specific situation or target. This image can be close to the reality, or otherwise unreal and idealized by the vampire, where its efficiency will depend on the intensity and consistency of the energy being projected. Unlike what is commonly assumed, this does not only allow the vampire to project an idea of terror, danger and lethal power, but also allows him to pass by an innocent human, weak and unaware, that can in many times be far more dangerous than a vampire projecting a strong and terrifying energy.

People will always feel affected by the aura projected by an Asetian, whether consciously or unconsciously, depending on their own metaphysical training, awareness and sensitivity. Despite flooding their aura with a specific energy, projection can also be done through the primary and secondary Shen Centers, using the voice and the look as tools to direct projection of the desired energy vibration. This kind of projection is not so subtle, and more direct, being used commonly with a desired target in mind. Although everyone is affected by the vampiric projection, its reaction will vary according to some variables, particularly the person's own way of interpreting energy, emotion and feelings. For example, when speaking, the voice can be infused with energy from the Throat Shen and secondary Shen of the mouth – that also includes tongue and lips – projecting a desired vibration, that can affect and manipulate the audience, both positively and negatively, depending on the intent and effectiveness of the procedure. When projecting through this mechanism, the infusing of energy in the voice can be heightened by the use of direct commands, which can be done through vocal messages or simple thoughts. It is not uncommon to see a vampire gain the attention of a desired target by the simple thought "See me. See me now." or to pass unnoticed from someone while thinking "Do not see me." and projecting that energy.[8] Thoughts, whether manifested by words or inside the mind, are energy. And this energy can be harnessed and directed towards our goals. That is the mechanism behind the practice of projecting, that when truly mastered can become something as simple and direct as the subtle vampiric commands previously stated. However, do not take these metaphysical techniques as an approach based on wishful thinking or placebo effects. The workings behind these mechanisms go far deeper and rely in one of the frameworks behind the Universe itself – the laws of attraction. This metaphysical hallmark can be applied and harnessed under a myriad of situations and towards any kind of goal, and it is an energy principal old as time itself. Like attracts like. Energy from one vibration attracts that same vibration. This concept is behind one of the major concepts in Kemeticism and Hermetics, the *Law of Thoth* – As Above, so Below. Being vampires creatures that can naturally project and manipulate abnormal quantities of energy, and do it in such an intense and powerful way, who better than them to equally attract the energies they want with much further ease? The Universe is their chosen realm. Energy is their weapon. The World bows and adapts to their own inner microcosm. Asetians are the children of the Gods after all...

Although inborn to Asetians, the ability to consciously project the Will dramatically increases after the awakening, which will make them able to produce vaster, denser and more effective energy fields. In some cases, an over developed shield can become an obstacle for the projection technique, since it ends up blocking some energy flow, interfering with the energy being projected, but that is not always the case. If the vampire infuses the energy from the shield with the desired effect, the shield can even become a tool, instead of an obstacle. This leads to a practice that is an offshoot of simple projecting, and a mix between this technique and shielding. It relies on the use of energy filters, to manipulate and affect people in the surroundings. *Filtering* consists precisely in the use of an energy shield, or even the aura field, and to infuse it with the intent and desired feel, that will affect people that come in contact with it. This energy, like the one used in any kind of projecting, will always carry the fingerprint of its owner, which can be a tracing element, used by anyone adept at energy work under the target of these practices, and another variable that will eventually affect the personal reaction of each individual to a selected projection. However, even though the fingerprint is present, the main reaction of the subject will usually be to the feel and vibration of the projected energy.

Manifesting

The ability to *manifest* is also inborn to vampires, although sometimes more complex to master, and in our days not as useful as projecting. It is another metaphysical tool that, although not as effective and powerful as projecting, does prove interesting in some specific situations, especially when in a life-threatening circumstance, like extreme weather and similar conditions.

Manifesting is the use of vital energy to increase physical and mental activities or change vital responses. This can be an increase in strength, stamina, speed, concentration and focus, or an increase or decrease of body temperature, heart rate, control of body fluids, sensory sensitivity and neurotransmission. The physical activities able to increase into stealth mode will change widely from vampire to vampire, depending on their energy metabolism and subtle body functioning. For example, someone that can dramatically increase physical strength, fueled by vital energy, might not be able to use energy to resist to extreme temperatures, or to improve concentration and reasoning, and so on. Each vampire has his own personal abilities concerning the applications of manifesting, and those might even change over time and are unpredictable, depending on the situation and global context.

Pushing yourself beyond the physically imposed limits might be an asset in some situations, but it certainly is something to use with extreme caution, because it is a poorly optimized process, meaning that it burns considerable amounts of energy to produce short bursts of performance. No one is able to manifest for long periods of time. It is a technique to be used in specific, short-term and extreme situations, which will easily drain out your own energy system, leaving the subtle body very vulnerable and exposed in the end.

Someone in the process of manifesting is said to be in *stealth* mode, although that definition is sometimes also used for a vampire consciously projecting, or with shields and awareness at its peaks. While the ability to project is a typical Viperine expertise, manifesting is a talent native to the Guardians. They unconsciously rely on this mechanism on a regular basis, especially when it comes to healing and health, where they increase their immune system and metabolism, achieving greater health states, higher healing rates and an important resistance to disease and outside influences. Despite these inborn tendencies of the Asetian bloodlines, both techniques can be mastered by the three lineages, on different levels and under dissimilar applications.

Inspiring

Vampires are truly inspiring creatures. They allure to anyone's senses and awaken their most inner desires, fears and emotions. As stated before, they are beings of chaos, which promote change and inspire creativity, allowing to surface many things in people otherwise inaccessible, unknown or unaware. This kind of inspiration, promoted by the vampire himself, is not always something obscure and unexplainable, but actually something purely metaphysical. Although many times done unconsciously, this vampiric trait can be learned, tweaked and mastered for conscious application. Being at its basics an offshoot of projecting, inspiring is a vampiric technique to activate or heighten certain emotions in others. The ability to inspire feelings, thoughts and emotions is also a very powerful tool, especially in social interaction, which should be used with caution.

The unconscious effect of inspiring is commonly seen in artists that find in vampires a source of inspiration, in gothic fashion and role-play vampires that have seen in the archetype a source of power and self-acceptance, and in the many people that criticize, condemn and fear the vampires. All of these are affected by their energies, and in this way *inspired* by them, whether it is positively and channeled to something productive like art, culture, philosophy and development of the self; or negatively channeled into anger, envy and frustration, that are also commonly seen manifested towards vampirism.

Oclumancy

The faculty to read the mind of others, feel what they are thinking and influence their thoughts is a renowned ability from the vampiric bloodlines. This field of magick and the occult, which deals with mind reading, thought influence and mind blocking is known as *oclumancy*. The oclumancy, although not highly known inside the occult studies, is an important practice inside the more elitist sects of witchcraft, which combines offensive and defensive techniques relying mainly in the use of energy links, tendrils and the Third Eye Shen.

The oclumancy group of studies uses an energy link, built from one Shen to another, and through this connection accesses and withdraws information from the conscious and unconscious mind of the target. Since an energy link works in both ways, it becomes clear how the process to influence and implant information can be done. While the process might look similar to typical telepathy, it is far more complex, reliable and should be seen more like a specific variety of psychic attack. Defensive mechanisms are also part of oclumancy, which consist primarily in blocking oclumancy attacks, effectively closing the mind or even feeding the attacker with wrong information conceived by the vampire and disguised as the real one. Most of these techniques are complex, and require a great control of the mind and energy manipulation. Despite being a potent attack tool when fully mastered, oclumancy is also not very subtle, being easily identified by an aware vampire. So, one of the more advanced developments of the practice is how to consciously use it without getting noticed. While using oclumancy with most of the human kind can be done virtually unnoticed, caution should be expected when applying these techniques with a vampire in target, that will easily get suspicious and probably detect the inbound signal and assume it as a psychic attack.

Vampires take their life force and energy fields very seriously, sometimes as something sacred to them. Any unauthorized or unrequested *touches* in their energies will be identified as direct attacks, many times seen by the vampire community as metaphysical rapes, and a lack of respect in this sort of situations can easily be reprehended by aggressive metaphysical responses and potent subtle attacks.

Anyone adept at metaphysics can learn techniques of oclumancy and develop this ability, but most of the experts on the field are people with an inborn talent to this specific occult field, many times manifested as an undeveloped gift since an early age.

Psychic Attack

One of the most discussed offensive arts from the vampire is their potent psychic attack. In almost all of the public literature about modern vampires, the main issue of debate is the danger of psychic attacks and how to defend from or escape them. This subject gave birth to a variety of defensive literature concerning the vampires and their dangers, being sometimes responsible for the proliferated fear from vampires in the occult society.

Psychic attack is, without doubt, a weapon. It is a metaphysical technique aimed to direct offensive attack. Its potency and effectiveness will depend on the skill of the attacker, his occult training and spiritual development, as well as the technique being used. When it comes to psychic attack, there are many techniques, options and variants on these procedures available to deliver the attack. Although most of them rely on the use of offensive tendrils, only one thing is always common to all techniques and variants of psychic attack – it all comes up to energy. Whether it is a direct offensive projection of highly intense energy to a Shen, able to stop the heart from beating, or a fast, malignant, energy drain through attached tendrils that will lead the victim to respiratory arrest and collapse, it is always a form of a psychic attack, under an occultist analysis.

An unawakened or untrained vampire will not be able to do an effective psychic attack, at least at the point of collapse or death of the victim. Actually, only highly developed vampires, with an intense and elitist training from a Master, can deliver death with their magickal *touch*. General drains won't have the necessary potency to result in physical death, even though they can slowly wear out the victim, and if prolonged for some time, result in unrecoverable damage to the sanity of the prey. However, most of the psychic attacks are not designed to use against potential donors or preys, but for usage against other magickal-aware creatures, that are not only able to activate defensive mechanisms against the attack, but also reply to it with effective and dangerous counter-attacks. Because of this, an attack should not only be designed in a way to be fast, effective and efficient, but also be applied with the minimum obvious impact, in a way to pass unnoticed to the prey as a way to slow down the activation of his subtle defenses. These are *stealth attacks,* which cannot be applied in every situation, but only in more premeditated attacks, where there is time to a more cautious planning and development of the technique.

Despite being an effective metaphysical weapon, a psychic attack also burns precious vital energy, which if not used wisely can come at a great expense to the practitioner. Many attacks are fueled by intense energy that is also important for the internal maintenance of the vampire's subtle system. Nearly all of the direct offensive techniques rely on our own vital energy to enhance the attack, whether it is an intense burst of energy being malignantly projected to a target, or the use of small, discrete tendrils being pushed into the victim's system allowing a flow of our own energy charged with a hazardous vibration into his system, resulting in a subtle breakdown. This is one of the reasons why psychic attacks should be used with caution and under a smart, responsible consideration. They easily wear down the personal vital force, and if done irresponsibly could simply leave the system more fragile and open to a powerful counter-attack in response to your own offensive moves. Actually, many attacks even enhance the potency of a counter-attack and give them free access through the attacker's own subtle defenses. Since some techniques rely on the use of tendrils and energy, which in practice ends up building a subtle link with the target, that can be used by an experienced vampire to exponentially increase the efficiency of a counter-attack. Using not only his own energy, but taking over the links built by the first offensive, can be a shortcut for bypassing the subtle firewalls of the opponent's shields and in this way hacking into their own energy system. Under this light, it comes obvious the importance of subtle tactics and advanced techniques in metaphysical warfare, dueling and confrontations. The vampiric and occult societies are not a world where the physically stronger rule, but a place where the evolved reign, and the not so intelligent, trickier and knowledgeable perish. It is a world of honor and deceit, where only the brighter can achieve greater things, and where the fools get easily drown by the never-ending flow of energy and time. It is the survival of the fittest and the stronger indeed, but those days where that meant a parallel with the physical are long gone, in the metaphysical society that means spiritual development and personal achievement, for the Self and for the group. A raw, rude muscle is no match for the genius and feline eye of the vampire. In fact, developed muscles and fat tissue are highly discouraged by the occult orders developing advanced metaphysical training. The reason for that is very simple – it degenerates energy flow. A high quantity of fat tissue, just like a highly developed muscular mass, are enemies of the energy practitioner, since they stagnate energy and restrain the desired energy flow to the practice of magick. Because of this, many occult trainings developed by the most experienced Masters also include a healthy diet, sometimes even extreme during the first times of training, to achieve the desired weight and body mass, not with beauty in mind, but ideal to the practice of magick and mastery of the varied occult disciplines, particularly energy manipulation. This was the reason why the myth of the vampire being a thin creature came to life, not that a vampiric creature needs to be thin and physically weak, but because of the importance of not having a developed muscular mass to the mastery of metaphysics, and how that has a direct impact in the abilities to defend and attack in the obscure occultist world.

The best way to prevent a psychic attack and defend from it is the already discussed use of energy shields. Although breakable and not always effective they still represent the strongest mechanism of direct passive defense against metaphysical attacks. A well-trained vampire will be able to drain down a shield, if he finds a way to directly connect to it, being one of the first steps if he wishes to attack the core of the target. However, and just like in almost every technique, there is a course of action against it, in this case being the use of malignant energy structures in the shield, making its drain a very difficult and dangerous process. Guardians do this effectively and in a very fast way, being another internal defensive mechanism of their subtle system, reason why their inborn energy shields are very complicated to tear down or bypass.

Also, do not expect psychic attacks just from vampires. There is a variety of otherkin creatures roaming this universe that are able to engage in offensive metaphysical attacks, and even a human well versed in the magickal arts can induce a potentially harmful attack. And not only the incarnated beings are able to subtly attack. Most of the creatures that live in the in-between world and the subtle realities, like the astral plane, can engage in offensive activities, from psychic attacks to vampiric drains, that everyone should always be aware of and effectively defend from, in order to keep themselves safe from harm and with their own vital energies intact.

FEEDING

Although the whole complexity and variety of metaphysical attacks can include vampiric feedings, with their potent and potentially harmful drains, this subject falls under a well deserved category of its own. Vampires are known to feed on life force. Their thirst for powerful, healthy and emotional energy is a well-known characteristic of nearly all of the vampiric creatures. However, the process of feeding is not something simple, but an occultist discipline that if mastered relies on advanced metaphysical concepts, techniques and abilities.

There are many different varieties of feeding, all dissimilar from each other, using differential techniques and resulting in distinctive effects in the vampire's energy system. A well-developed vampire will learn how to consciously use most of the feeding variants, but will never master all of them. That will depend on his inborn abilities and personal taste, as well as the energy metabolism from his lineage and personal subtle genetics of the vampire himself.

Thirst

Thirst is the expression used for levels of energy need, experienced by the subtle system, and it can be simply translated as the hunger for vital force. The thirst is a phenomenon exclusively vampiric, which is not felt by other species with a sane subtle system, and can be experienced under different levels of need. These levels can range from a minor need, that can be simply replenished by ambient feeding and elemental energy, almost without interfering with the stability of the energy system, to high and demanding energy needs, that depend on direct feedings, normally with contact and deep drains, to rebalance the whole system: subtle, physical and mental.

The use of the word thirst to describe the feelings of energy craving comes from the nature of the vital energy itself, being a metaphysical and alchemical fluid from the ethereal realm, reason why making it parallel to liquids is more intuitive and metaphysically correct than simply calling it hunger, connecting it to the ingestion of something solid.

The experience of thirst can be felt in a myriad of situations and feelings, which change from vampire to vampire. The feelings are quite stronger and more severe in Viperines, because of their highly developed energy metabolism, but are present in every vampire, manifesting through different patterns and having individual consequences. For example, the ability that Guardians have to keep their energy reserves to a minimum and still be able to enforce powerful actions, might lead to situations of chronic depression if allowed to endure for long periods of time. In some of these cases the thirst can simply manifest by feelings of sadness and sorrow. Also, the typical antisocial behaviors of the Guardians can become a feeding obstacle, because of the scarce direct interaction with humans, making it hard to gather enough viable situations to feed efficiently, making them known for being the most elitist feeders of all, having a minimum amount of donors, and commonly just being interested in engaging in direct feeding from someone very intimate to them and with a sacred energy bond, like another Asetian.

Ambient Feeding

The techniques of ambient feeding are the less optimized and efficient of all, but are the easier ones to engage in nearly every situation, without any direct consequence or metaphysical violation of another one's energy field. Ambient feeding relies on draining the energy of a confined space, like a room, so the energy being absorbed not only has a lower vibration, as it lacks a defined energy fingerprint, since it is detached from a living being. Most of these energies are no longer vital force – Ka – but residual energy, projected by individuals, detached from the aura of living beings and released in active emotional activity. Because of this, the feeding is only effective in places of energy concentration, that can range from a bar, a cinema or a concert, where people use to gather; to religious places like churches and temples, where more intense residual energy can usually be found. This is one of the reasons why real vampires, unlike the ones in fiction and myth, actually are fond of places like churches, mosques and temples, because of its usually charged ambient energy.

The nature of the residual energy and its low vibration does not prove to be a reliable feeding source to every vampire. Actually some don't even deal well with this mix of floating energies from humans, depending from the dominant vibration. Like the Viperine lineage, that can even be weakened in crowded places precisely because of that metaphysically polluted environment. However, in most cases, an ambient feed will never be able to replenish a low energy level, and can only be used in situations of minor need. Ambient feeding does not create any subtle links in the process, since it relies on detached residual energy that floats around in the chosen feeding environment, which can be an important variable in some situations.

Indirect Feeding

Indirect feeding, also known as social feeding, is one of the most common and used forms of energy draining. Whether antisocial or not, everyone interacts with other creatures, being them humans and otherkin. Virtually any situation of interaction with another person can be harnessed for feeding, without any need of direct physical contact. This is called indirect feeding.

The process involves the extension of the vampire's own tendrils to the victim, and the piercing of their aura, creating a draining link that allows the energy to flow into the vampire's subtle system. The wound left by this sort of attack might not be severe, if done with caution, and will heal quickly. However if the drain is done more violently, or the tendril is injected more deeply, the wound in the aura can take more time to heal properly.

Also, since all emotions, and many thoughts, heighten and project energy, it is also possible for the vampire to manipulate a kind of situation when interacting with others, that will induct a projection of energy that is then promptly absorbed by him, being another form of social feeding. This is also obvious in situations where a vampire projects himself into a crowd or social interaction, and drains the audience by their attention, admiration or respect. Particularly the Viperines are most acclaimed at this sort of projection and manipulative drain, despite being the lineage that is far more adept of the high-demanding drains like direct contact, sexual and deep feeding.

Being indirect feeding one of the techniques that fuels the system of the vampire with vital force from another living being, it results in a weakened subtle system for the victims, that despite the subtle wound left on the aura, are also left with their energy reserves running lower. The human subtle system will slowly replenish their vital energy by their natural link to universal energy, and be rebalanced in time. Only if a drain is too violent, it can create additional complications or put the life of the prey at risk, which is ultimately rare in this sort of feeding. Indirect feeding results in weak energy links attached to the prey that, in most cases, just linger for a few minutes to a few hours, before the energy of the link dissipates.

In these feeding techniques donors are rarely involved, being the reason why the word victim and prey are more commonly used when referring to indirect and social feeding. Most of the drains with a consenting donor are done using contact feeding techniques, and other variants that involve a far more deep drain. Indirect feeding is very useful in vampiric hunting, where the vampire leaves his lair in the hunt for preys to satisfy his inner energy lust. In those hunts for unwilling and unaware preys can also be used other more intimate techniques, that will be addressed in the next topics.

Contact Feeding

This is one of the most typical forms of feeding between consenting donors. Contact feeding implies physical contact to activate the subtle link from where the energy will be drained. Commonly, this physical contact remains during the process of feeding, but in cases where more discretion is needed, or the drain is supposed to pass unnoticed by the victim, then a subtle, single and fast touch on someone's skin can be enough to plug the tendril into the aura and then simply walk away, stretching the link and pulling energy out through it. Some level of mastery in energy work is required to attain the kind of concentration needed to correctly perform some of these techniques. However, this is not the most pleasant way to contact feed, and is more generally used in stealth situations, like vampire hunting. In more consentient and profound situations it is possible to rely in metaphysical procedures very specific to the Asetian kin, where a prolonged contact is more advised.

Although more efficient in the form of deep, sexual and tantric feeding, in contact feeding it is possible to engage in a form of energy exchange, that can benefit both vampires and donors. It is an advanced mechanism of draining that allows an exchange of energy in a way that does not only intensely feed the vampire, as heightens the energy flowing inside the donor's subtle system, increasing its quality, vibration and density. It allows for echoes and vibrations of the Violet Flame to touch the donor's Crown Shen, empowering and refreshing his energy system, while at the same time promotes the cycling of Ka and the breaking of stagnation centers. This feeding technique, which can be applied in different feeding variants, is always a blessing for the donor that is willingly giving his energy to the vampire, creating a more intimate bond, reason why it is not practiced with just about any donor. Actually, this technique is only fully efficient if done within the Asetian family, because of the natural energy rapport between Asetians, but can also be done at a smaller extent with non-Asetian donors as well. This sacred practice is called *Concordia*. The word has its roots in the Latin, and it means agreement, harmony and union. Being a specifically Asetian draining technique, Concordia is not a feeding variant of its own, since it can be applied under different kinds of vampiric feeding.

The subtle links created during contact feeds are stronger than the ones forged in the techniques of indirect feeding, with its roots going deeper into the inner layers of the aura, surface of the Shen Centers or even the energy system itself. These links can take a considerable amount of time to dissipate, and if enforced with thoughts, emotions or by frequent drains, can be allowed to intensify and root into the system, making them far more difficult to dissipate or to be removed.

Deep Feeding

Without entering the realm of sexually inducted feedings, the most powerful and intimate kind of draining is the deep feeding. It is a very intense variant of vampiric feeding, which relies in draining not from the aura, or the surface of a Shen, but from the kernel of the energy system. This is not easy to accomplish, and needs the consent of the donor as a prerequisite to be succeeded.

Draining the energy from the roots of another's essence gives access to a realm of things, since the energy being accessed and absorbed is not only very intense, but also very personal to the individual. It is possible that during the process, thoughts, feelings and emotions pass to the vampire, allowing him to feel what the donor is feeling, and sometimes even to see throughout the unconscious mind of the donor. It is a process to engage only with someone with whom a great level of trust was achieved. But that is not the only danger of deep feeding. This profound variant of feeding creates a subtle link with the donor that simply does not vanish quickly or easily, like the ones coined in the previously addressed forms of feeding. The energy links created in the context of deep feeding linger for a long time, and if properly enforced, can remain active for a whole lifetime or even longer. These strong and intimate links can have a myriad of consequences, from empathy and even telepathy, to the souls feeling drawn to each other in future incarnations. That is something to be seen with great caution, because a donor and friend today, might not be the same tomorrow, or even worse and unpredictable in the next life. So engaging in deep feeding should be done with a highly conscious mind. In real world analysis, this ends up not being a very problematic issue, since a deep feed is not something easy to accomplish, that relies in advanced metaphysical techniques and a great deal of control, not every vampire is able to deep feed from who he wants and when he wants, without a high dose of spiritual and personal evolution.

Sexual Feeding

Sexual, along with tantric, are some of the most intimate variants of vampiric feeding. It relies heavily on physical contact and energy links established through the Sexual Shen Centers. If the practice is maintained between passionate and loving couples, it can become a marvelous metaphysical experience, rooting the feelings of the partners and increasing the sexual sensations. The deepness of the drain can be potentially high in the course of sexual feeding, in parallel with the deep feeds, bounding the souls to each other and potentiating a very intimate energy exchange, that can prove to be tremendously sustaining. The energy exchanged during a sexual feed is naturally heightened and condensed, not only because of the intimacy of the sexual activity itself, but also because of the emotional charge and sensations attached to it. The whole procedure and direct Shen connection is very different from the other forms of feeding. Because of all these reasons, sexual feeding is something to be done preferentially with someone with a great, intimate bond, in relations of love and not just a regular willing donor. However, it is possible to engage in sexual feeding without any feelings of love and great emotional bond. But despite what might be believed, or making believe, in the vampiric society, the effectiveness of this kind of feeding with a simple donor, aware of it or not, without an attached emotional relation, can not simply be done by just any vampire, requiring a great deal of spiritual development, energy mastery, control and a nice quota of knowledge, that is not simply inborn. Regularly, this kind of situations can only be mastered by the Elders and a few talented exceptions. And most of the Elders do not even engage in these activities with people without a strong bond, nor endorse its practice. Without this level of development and mastery, the physical steps up, gaining control of the activity, ending up in just a sexual relation, and not a metaphysical experience of a sexual feed. The physical body is a system of impulses, and it is not always is easy to overcome that rooted influence and to center in the subtle, but far more beautiful, part of it.

Usually the subtle links initiated during sexual feeds are very deep and intimate, similar to the ones created during the deep feeds. However, that will depend greatly on the kind of sexual feed being used. Like explained before, if the sexual feed is being engaged between someone without a deep bond with the vampire, not in a love relationship, then the resulting energy links will be far weaker, and easier to dissipate or break. On the other hand, like in the case of deep feeding, the links created out of an emotional bond and true profound relation, will result in a very strong connection, with deep roots in the subtle system, that can linger for a very long time.

Sexual feeding is the vampiric draining technique most connected to the concept of *energy lust*, extensively attached to the vampire. The Asetian is a creature of powerful energy, characterized by his inborn need to intake energy from outer sources, particularly the charged and heightened variants of Ka, to stabilize his own energy system, maintaining it healthy, and empowering himself, using that same energy to manifest in the form of magick – the vampiric powers. This craving for living and vibrant energy, when satisfied in the form of a deep drain, but especially in a highly emotional and even erotic feed, like the sexual drains, can be seen as a form of lust, particular of the vampire kind, and more intense than anything that can be humanly felt.

Tantric Feeding

Tantric feeding is an offshoot of sexual feeding. Its ability is sometimes inborn to Guardians, and its mastery is almost exclusive to their lineage. The process of tantric feeding is an advanced technique, which implies the feeling of pleasure, emotional and sexual, from the practitioner, without the need of being physically inducted. This means that the vampire is feeling sexual pleasure, but he is only giving it physically to someone, a donor or another vampire, without actively receiving the same physical stimulus. This is possible through a metaphysical mechanism where the vampire drains in a very special way the heightened energy being released by the partner in the course of sexual stimulation. The way that the vampire drains, absorbs and processes this energy, allows for the feelings to intensely pass from the donor to himself, allowing for him to feel considerable amounts of pleasure from giving sexual pleasure to the partner. If this technique is correctly applied, the energy being absorbed is so intense and the process is so efficient, that it allows the vampire to project his own heightened energy from the pleasure echoes being felt in his own body. So, if the partner is another vampire, it is possible for him to also drain this energy from the other vampire engaging the tantric feed, while he is receiving the full pleasure of the sexual intercourse. Being this one of the special cases, with energetic and metaphysical benefits to both intervenient vampires, it can be seen as one of the specific variants of *Concordia*, the particularly Asetian way of mutual beneficial drains between vampires. These techniques can only work between partners with a strong emotional bond, preferably a love relation and ideally within the Asetian family.

Being tantric feeding a derived form of sexual feeding, that could only be applied between experienced partners with a great deal of trust and emotional bond, the links resulting from this kind of vampiric feeding are parallel with the ones created in sexual drains, with the fact that the nature of the link itself and its positioning in the subtle system can result in some way in an addictive practice, for both practitioners.

Astral Feeding

Not all forms of feeding have a physical component, as was already explained, but some don't even rely on a nearby presence of the desired target to actively feed from it. One of the most common variants of that kind of draining, many times also seen as an efficient form of psychic attack, is the astral feeding.

An astral feeding occurs in another plane, outside of the physical realm, known as the astral, that is part of the subtle reality. The soul of the vampire, although connected to the body by the silver cord, is not inside of it, as it usually is during the other forms of feeding. The vampire enters a meditative state, and projects himself out of his body, into the astral plane, roaming this realm in the search for a prey. Usually the selected target should be asleep, to facilitate the draining of the vampire, but it is not a requisite to successfully drain via astral projection. Many people while sleeping are actually roaming the astral realm, finding in their own dreams gateways out of the dreamspace and into the subtle reality. This allows for the dreamer to interact with other souls, some might be also asleep, but others are not. The vampires, known to master the subtle planes and other realities, use this kind of technique to feed from targets that might not be so easily accessible in the physical realm, like someone that lives far away from them. Although moderately efficient, even if done properly, the astral feeding is not as enriching, nor as empowering, as the already mentioned variants of contact, deep and sexual feeding. Even though the vampire is roaming in a full energy form, the links created during this kind of drain are not that strong, and can easily dissipate in time, if not allowed to root, from situations like constant feeding from the same source.

Despite being a known technique at the disposal of an awakened vampire, it is also a common experience, manifested unconsciously by the creatures that are vampiric in nature. More commonly between unawakened vampires, many have already experienced an unconscious astral feed during sleep. This might not be something obvious to recognize to someone inexperienced with dream work and astral projection. When a vampire is on low energy, the craving increases and the true *thirst* manifests, but if because of any situation he is not allowed to feed, his unconscious mind will start looking for viable options to restore the lost balance of his energy system. In these cases, a common solution is to astral feed during the sleeping time, many times doing it unconsciously, out of instinct. Being these cases a perfect example of the predatory nature of the vampire.

In the case of unconscious astral feed it is possible for the vampire to find himself feeding of someone that he would not willingly do, but for whatever reason their unconscious mind found it a viable prey. Although this situation can be uncomfortable for the vampire, it can be corrected with learning some skills of basic energy work and astral travel. Sometimes a simple shielding technique with the proper programmed shields can be enough to control this situation, that although far more typical in the unawakened, also happens between awakened and developed vampires.

Ritual Feeding

A not very thoroughly discussed form of feeding in our days is the draining of vital force using ritual magick. With the aid of magickal procedures and sigil manipulation, ritual is a renowned powerful tool to any vampire. More commonly used to the change of reality according to the vampire's own desires, the ritualistic side of magick can also be used to enforce a bunch of vampiric activities, like feeding. Ritual magick, even though different in theory from other metaphysical practices, like direct energy work, ends up being pure energy manipulation as well, but this time done in an indirect way. Known in the vampiric subculture as a reliable form of destructive magick, but also commonly used to personal achievement and development of the Self in the practices of high magick, ritual is one of the least used forms of feeding.

One of the greatest tools in ritual magick, and so likely in ritual feeding, is the use of sigils – magickal seals with hidden symbols of power. Most of the sigils used by the vampire are ancient in nature, with an obscure meaning, many times only known to the practitioner. The Asetians are also known for their expertise in the sacred art of sigil creation and mastery in the use of this force. So, it is common for the vampire to use a myriad of different sigils within his magickal practices, with varied meanings, associated mantras and spells, having at his disposal a complex set of tools in order to use and manipulate. The sigil is far more than a symbol. It gains life and becomes an entity of its own. It embodies a specific energy, charge, feel, and symbolism, representing a very detailed archetype, created by the vampire that gave it life, almost like a corporeal elemental that becomes a servitor of its master.

Not being one of the most efficient ways of vampiric feeding, in a sense that the energy is indirectly drained, and so it is not as heightened and vibrant, ritual feeding has the advantage that does not create subtle links attached to the energy body. This is true because of the mechanism used in this kind of feeding, which being indirect, does not allow the attachment and rooting of any kind of energy links, where the mechanism itself works as a kind of metaphysical firewall, between the vampire and his prey. The advantage of this kind of approach is not merely the absence of subtle links, but also the difficulties imposed in the tracking down of an attack of this kind, being sometimes impossible to trace down, if done with the proper care. A direct energy drain, using the before mentioned energy techniques, is far more aggressive, being a lot easier to be noticed by the aware victims, if having any kind of metaphysical training or sensitivity to the subtle and energetic reality. But despite these obvious disadvantages, this remains still the preferred kind of attacks and energy draining procedures used by vampires, mainly because of the more natural course of action attached to it, that allures to the inborn predatory nature of an Asetian, and allows for a whole more intimate and profound way to directly feed from living beings.

In common day practice, ritual feeding is many times not used as a form of a sustaining drain for the health, sanity and empowerment of the vampire, but more as an effective way to psychic attack. Ritual drains can prove to be devastating if done in parallel with the aid of destructive magickal sigils, used in the dark arts of the offensive vampiric magick.

Blood Feeding

Blood is a powerful, although polemic, tool in metaphysics. The vampiric feed through the ingestion of living blood is one of the most taboo subjects in the occultist society, despite being the most commonly explored side of the vampire in fiction.

Blood is a highly charged physical substance, infused with the vital force of its host. The reason for this particularity of the blood fluid is due to the alignment between the physical blood vessels and the subtle energy vessels – the meridians – and can be easily explained through the study of subtle anatomy. Because of this, the blood and its binding to vital energy has been connected with the vampire and vampiric practices for thousands of years. But it is not only for feeding that the blood is used in metaphysics, but also as a powerful tool in magick, particularly in the ancient dark arts. Blood is used in ritual, sacred pacts, bindings and many other forms of magick.

For the vampire, blood has always been a vehicle of life force and also a point of focus to an effective drain. The vampiric attacks by the means of a blood drain have become so intricately rooted in the human subconscious mind that they help to parallel the vampire with danger and terror. Although these feedings are represented in fiction by a messy attack, with large bite wounds and loads of blood, reality is far from this surreal representation. Blood feeding is not done through the ingestion of high quantities of blood, but just small amounts of it. A vampire does not drink glasses filled with blood, nor drains someone until the person gets *dry*, which is purely fiction. Despite the situations described in the new-age vampire lifestyle subculture, where some self-proclaimed vampires state that they drink a lot of blood, frequent blood bars, and eat crude bloody meat, to sustain their supposed vampiric need, that is all merely ridiculous on a metaphysical approach. Dead blood does not contain any life force at all. So the ingestion of blood as vampiric feeding only has some metaphysical effect if done directly from the victim, or donor. Energy quickly dissipates from the blood, if left exposed out of the body and not in contact with the subtle field of the host. That is why the eating of unprocessed and bloody meat does not feed a vampire, in any case. And besides this metaphysical incongruence, an Asetian does not rely on animal energy, and it does not simply absorb just any kind of essence, being tremendously elitist from who they feed and how they feed, giving a major importance to the purity of their own vital force – the Asetian sacred essence.

Despite all the before mentioned, the blood feeding among vampires exists, and so does unwilling blood attacks. However, the most common form of blood feeding is between consenting donors. A small amount of blood is sufficient for a reasonable quantity of energy to be drained from the donor. Although the blood feeding has a very physical component, being that the blood itself, it is not independent from metaphysical work, relying on subtle techniques along the drain, to efficiently absorb the vital force from the blood and process it in the energy system. Even though feeding is something inborn in every vampire that can be developed in an intuitive way, the proper method to efficiently do it, in a way to empower his own Self and to allow the inner powers to manifest, fueling them with the captured energy, is something that can be only accomplished and mastered with proper training from a master.

During a blood feed, both the physical and subtle essences of the donor get mixed with the one from the vampire, inside the vampire's own body. This energy mingling is also one of the reasons that lead the Asetians to only blood feed from highly special donors, striving for the purity of their sacred essence. Because of this interfusion of energies, the subtle links created in this kind of feeding tend to be quite strong, and particularly hard to break.

Blood is a metaphysically binding substance. It connects people and draws them together. It is something always taken with a great respect by an Asetian, who tries to treat with honor, care and respect this physical substance infused with vital force, and who's blood is seen as sacred.

In the end, it is important to keep in mind that although blood is definitely entwined with the vampire history and magick, its use for feeding purposes is not always a most important factor. With the vast metaphysical tools at the disposal of the vampire, and with all the strength and power of the direct energy manipulation skills, blood ends up being just another option for the advanced vampire. Like some unawakened and undeveloped vampires, many highly evolved Asetians and Elders don't even blood feed at all, as a personal taste and option, meaning that the use of blood-based techniques are not in any way a mean to hierarchize or categorize a vampire or his personal growth and spiritual evolution. What the vampire truly needs, and craves for, is pure, intense and high-quality vital force, the inner energy of the living beings, known by the Elders as Ka. This is something far more powerful, intense and deep, but at the same time more subtle, obscure and complex, than blood. That is the only true essence of the soul. Blood is the life, but only because Ka is life itself.

Donors

An energy donor to a vampire, an exclusively vampiric relation, is a subject that could be so extensively developed at the point of writing a whole book about it. However, we will only skim the surface of the subject within the contents of this book.

In Asetianism, the relation between donor and vampire is almost sacred, and of major importance. It is something to honor without question. Actually, sometimes a donor of an Asetian master ends up becoming an apprentice of this vampire, learning the secret arts of the Gods, usually entitled as a *Dark Apprentice*. But there are many kinds of donors, and not all are of such a high importance and intimate to the vampire.

A vampire that exclusively feeds from his donor is something rare, and even impracticable in the case of vampires with a highly developed energy metabolism. The most complete and reliable option usually is to have a close donor – if available – for more intimate and deep feeds, and rely on vampiric hunting for casual drains and energy cycling. This can happen socially, while hanging out, and even during professional activity. The awakening and metaphysical training gives the vampire the option to choose when and how to feed. It is also uncommon to find an Asetian with many donors, preferring to trust that honorable exchange to only one or two persons, close to their relations, which they know well. Some don't even have any fix donors at all, whether it is from the lack of an ideal being for the *position*, or because of personal choice. It is inevitable that a recurrent donor gets bound to the vampire, sometimes for the rest of his life, in cases of regular deep feeds. Subtle links forged with donors are far stronger and powerful than the ones created in just an ordinary feed, and the holiness of this exclusively vampiric relation is something to honor at all times.

ADVANCED MAGICK

T his last chapter of the Asetian Bible is far from being the most profound and complex in what comes to comprehension and understanding, but it is the most advanced in terms of practical magick. This last text approaches different practices and techniques that require a certain level of mastery in energy and spiritual development, some of which are not exclusively vampiric.

Some concepts that will be addressed in the next pages are very advanced and require a great mastery and dedicated training from a specialized master, like the case of *Subtle Surgery*. Others are mainly advanced Asetian knowledge and magick, as the techniques involving *Metaphysical Tattooing*, which is sacred metaphysical knowledge, only mastered by the Elders.

Banishing

To magically repel someone, physically or from the subtle realms, by the means of magickal powers, is known as banishing, and it is a metaphysical practice under the spectrum of energy work. Banishing is more commonly used with spirits and other beings from the subtle realm. A typically offensive creature or subtle parasite will require a banishing to leave you alone. Sometimes this banishing will require some amount of struggle with the entity, and some offensive magick might be helpful in more resilient cases. If we are dealing with a being without self-awareness, the banishing should present no trouble. But the creatures from the other side can prove to be quite powerful and capable of considerable amounts of damage in incarnated beings, so when a banishing is engaged, some caution should be taken in consideration.

The banishing techniques will become particularly useful when someone starts to develop his awareness of the subtle reality and engaging in practical energy work. This usually draws closer some creatures from the other realms and gives the practitioner enough sensitivity to become aware of other presences and beings. Also, with the development of the Self potentiated by the Asetian training, religion and metaphysical practices, the energy of the initiate undergoes deep internal changes, becoming healthier, far denser and with a higher vibration. This high-quality energy and powerful vital force of the Asetian kind certainly draws attention from the subtle reality, and is highly desired and envied by a myriad of other creatures, even humans. This is one of the reasons why there will be an increased amount of contacts and sightings of disembodied beings from the point someone starts to interact with magick and energy, increasing its quality and indirectly purifying it by spiritual evolution and metaphysical practice.

A banishing cannot only be applied to other beings, but to energy in general. This is especially useful if someone desires to plunge a specific type of energy and vibration from his presence or from a particular location.

Unlike when directly banishing another being, that commonly relies on straight energy manipulation, the banishing of undesired energies is sometimes done in a ritual manner, making use of more ritualistic magickal techniques, that although not used in a direct creature banishing, can certainly be used as well when banishing someone from afar.

Binding

Binding is an extreme magickal practice and requires a great deal of mastery in energy work and personal power. This highly offensive technique is all about control. It allows the practitioner to force someone at their own will, from a physical incarnated being to a subtle entity from the astral, and more commonly to bind them to something. This is very effective against subtle parasites and other unwanted disembodied creatures from the astral plane, but it is also very dangerous. Binding a creature to a vessel creates a metaphysical prison, making it far more offensive and hateful towards yourself once it gets loose, if it ever comes to that. Any binding will definitely incentive the target to pursue you for your entire life, and sometimes even beyond. Binding another being will also require that your Will and power is superior to his own, or else there is always the danger of the target striking back and trying to bind yourself, and rest assured, it will try.

The techniques used for binding are considerably advanced, and demand a great deal of focus and high amounts of energy. One of the most powerful tools for binding is the use of magical sigils, being a potent way to enforce the binding and imprison the target inside a vessel, or confine him in the desired place.

When it comes to the Asetian history, the use of potent binding techniques was applied during the great epic battles of the ancient times, by both of the sides involved. The binding of the extraordinary powers and creatures unleashed in these days was many times a great tactical advantage, but the power required to wield it was confined only to a few.

Despite its use in battle, the use of magickal binding is a considerable choice when it comes to dealing with a persistent being, more commonly subtle parasites that will recursively return after each defeat. However, the use of a binding should never be taken lightly, and always used as responsible choice done as a last resource to deal with a metaphysical problem. It should never be used to deal with any mundane or physical world problem, as well as any other powerful magickal tool. Also keep in mind that every binding should ever be watched closely and carefully, for there is no definitive binding, and even the most powerful ones that endure for lifetimes eventually collapse and are defeated. If a subtle entity is trapped somewhere by a binding enchantment, it will not give up until it breaks the spell, or is set loose. So making a prisoner of a malignant creature is always a subject of extreme caution.

There is an offshoot of regular offensive binding. This sometimes called Empowerment Binding, or Talismanic Binding, is a variant of the binding techniques that allows the Asetian to bind a created servitor, a desired entity, and even a willing creature or power, to a magickal tool or talisman. Commonly this kind of binding is used with a magickal wand for regular use on the field, or with an amulet for an everyday use by its bearer. The use of this practice can enforce an object with a great deal of power and energy, like the long envied talismans of the Asetians and their powerful magickal wands that have become legend.

Disembodied Beings and Subtle Parasites

We live in an obscure and mystical world, full of life and full of magick. Even though most of the non-magickal folk cannot perceive, we all live surrounded by creatures. Those who in this moment taste the lustfulness of flesh and bitterness of mortality are the currently incarnated souls: humans, vampires and otherkin. But not all beings are incarnated at the present time.

Actually, a far vaster range of creatures is not incarnated in our days, and some do not even possess the ability and blessing of incarnation – the physical mortality. These non-incarnated beings, known as the disembodied, roam the subtle worlds and the astral plane, usually as energy alone, some not even sentient but others quite aware and powerful. The interaction with these beings from the other side is not only possible, but also frequent and common, although not everyone possesses the sensibility and awareness to become receptive to those interactions. The kind of creatures out there is very diverse and exists under a complexity of planes and manifestations, some of which are not fully understandable to most of us. A disembodied being can also be the soul of a dead person, incarnated in the past, but now in the subtle realm, commonly called a spirit. Not all of these beings from the other realms are safe; in fact some can become quite dangerous under the right circumstances and will violently attack. Some beings from the subtle world can have vampiric behaviors, draining the life force of the incarnated ones and sometimes attaching to their energy system and keeping like that for long periods of time, slowly feeding from the energy of the host, making him weaker and vulnerable. These beings are called subtle parasites, and sometimes can give a considerable amount of work to get rid of. However, that is not a reason to become paranoid. Many people start to parallel everything they feel and sense with the subtle realm and metaphysics, sometimes in situations where it can be simply explained by normal rationality, even when that is not the obvious option. That is something that should be taken in consideration at all times in our spiritual journey; involvement with magick and the occult is not a reason to run away from science and rationality. Wishful thinking, surreal fantasy and pretending is most of all a giant step into oblivion, the path to personal recession, instead of the spiritual Asetian hallmark: the development of the Self and the conquering of our true abilities while accepting the lost inner nature. On the top of this, subtle parasites and aggressive disembodied beings exist. Daemons and other perils in the subtle realm, as well as the physical world, exist. We should not run away from it, nor turn our backs at it. But we should not make of every guess a case of belief. Simply keep in mind that these things are real, the danger exists, but it is not that common as an everyday occurrence. Most of the people never had any true problems with a subtle parasite. Be aware of it, not obsessed by it.

If a true case is detected, whether it is a persistent subtle parasite or an aggressive being from the astral plane, there are many ways to deal with the situation. The most direct course of action is simple: reinforce your subtle defenses and engage in metaphysical attack. The experience, power and Will of all the intervenient will be decisive, if it has come to this. But keep in mind that, as beings of energy alone, they are in their native realm. Manipulating and dealing with energy is their way of life. However, most of the times the invasive beings from the other realms are more of a nuisance than a real danger, and can be simply drawn away with magickal cleansing techniques, grounding or a minor banishing. The most resilient and problematic cases can be dealt with a full banishing, with all the consequences that have been already described in relation to this metaphysical approach. Extreme cases of physical death caused by a subtle being are most of all unlikely, and nearly touching the realms of impossibility. Which does not mean that dying in a metaphysical battle from a subtle attack is not something very real.

Servitors

The creation of a servitor is a highly advanced form of magick. A servitor is a being of pure energy that is created by the sorcerer. This creature will be controlled by the practitioner and can have many functions. There are two different kinds of servitors: the low servitors and the royal servitors.

The creation of low servitors is part of the general knowledge that can be found within the occult literature on this subject, practiced by witches and wizards in ritual magick. This servitor is built upon intent, directed Will and energy, and is bound to its creator and his life force, in a symbiotic bond of reciprocation, where the being serves the master in exchange for being sustained by his energy. The liability and endurance of the servitor will depend on the Will and power of the practitioner and will always be a very energy-consuming process. Well-created servitors by masters in this art can be quite powerful and become very dangerous. Also, this kind of servitors should be bound to a specific object by the means of ritual magick, or otherwise it will easily dissipate and become unstable. Keep in mind that once a low servitor is created and bounded to the desired object, it cannot be changed into another one and it will be dependent from that same vessel forever, with no exceptions. Regularly, servitors can be dealt just like any other form of subtle being, like if it was a disembodied soul. However, it is important to be aware that this is not a sentient creature, and it is bound to its master and wielded by his Will.

Very different are the royal servitors, sometimes called only servitors by the Asetians. Although bounded to its creator and master, like any other servitor, the royal servitors have the possibility to be changed from one object to another. They are also quite more sentient and aware than regular servitors. These creatures are exclusively created by the means of Asetian magick, and rely on a sacred knowledge that only the Elders are said to possess. This kind of servitors is closely related with the subtle nature of the infamous Asetian wands and sacred talismans. The use of a magickal name in those metaphysical objects and the legend that they possess life and Will of their own is related with the ability of the Asetians in the creation of other forms of servitors, from a darker nature and different from what would be the common definition of a servitor by ritual magick practitioners. The Asetian servitors can be bound to someone that was not their creator, commonly called their master, but this bound can only be done by the Elder who created it. Although intimately bound to their master, these servitors will have an energy and subtle field of their own, and they will not drain out their masters, although being able to be fueled by them to achieve certain goals or to manifest some kind of powers, as they can also fuel their masters with specific vibrations and powers as well. They will usually be bound to a magickal wand or a personal talisman from an Asetian, like a jewel, and can only be wielded by their power. Unlike low servitors, this kind of subtle beings can be bound to another object in the future, for example if the wand is crushed in battle or the talisman is physically, but not metaphysically, destroyed. The Asetian will always be able to change the physical host of his servitor if his inner nature and existence survives. There is no servitor that is fully immortal, but they can prove to be hardy and even quite powerful, where some are even able to linger for more than a human lifetime. A well-mastered and developed servitor is very praised among vampires and can be very useful in different situations. Sometimes they linger from one incarnation to another, always following their master, who would bind them to a new magickal object in every new incarnation. Others are object of envy and reason of plotting, treason and war. Powerful servitors and their sacred objects have been quested in the metaphysical history of the Asetians, and sometimes even desired among opposing empires and considered a treasure beyond count, treated like one of their most precious values. If the talisman is not destroyed or the servitor within set loose from it, he will linger on bound to that object. The secret to wield the powers of a stolen talisman with a servitor has been thoroughly searched by humans, otherkin and even other vampiric bloodlines, which also constitutes a reason for metaphysical warfare in the past. Some of these sacred objects have caused people to go mad and become completely destroyed and consumed by it, loosing themselves in the deepness of the void that awaits an Asetian servitor without his master. This also explains the importance given to some talismans, amulets and magickal wands from the Asetian people, who treat them like sacred objects, with an identity of their own.

The use of talismans with royal servitors by the Asetians in the ancient world also gave birth to different myths and beliefs, being one of the most famous, the existence of *Genies* – a term for the word *Jinn* in Arabic. These beings, in the Arabian mythology, were a race of supernatural creatures that, just like the Asetian servitors, were usually bound to some special object and could be wielded by their masters, since they would not obey to just about anyone. They were also very feared because of their mighty supernatural powers, which was derived from the use of royal servitors by the Asetians in the time of the Epic Wars. They were also thought to be invisible to humans and having an identity of their own, which is very close to the far older Asetian definition of royal servitor. Also in the Arabian mythology and their later Islamic interpretations, the Jinn was thought to be made out of fire, and the Asetian Servitors are made out of pure Violet Flame, interpreted by many as the Divine Fire. Later in history, because of the invisible and subtle nature of the Asetian Servitor, along with its great metaphysical power in battle and other offensive situations, it started to be paralleled with the concept of Daemon, that is a whole different rank of subtle creatures, which only in some particular cases can be, in fact, considered high-class royal servitors.

Constructs

The use of constructs is a typically vampiric form of energy manipulation, but not exclusive to their kin. It can range from simple, straightforward constructs, to highly complex structures, requiring very advanced magickal techniques. The application and creation of constructs is infinite, being a very powerful and useful tool for any sorcerer.

In a very basic way, constructs are subtle structures built out of energy. The energy manipulator uses specific metaphysical techniques that allow him to direct energy, mold it into the desired form, charge it with the desired vibration and then *consolidate* it, making it coherent and harder to dissipate. However, no matter how powerful the wizard is, energy is dynamic and will always dissipate and degrade over time. So any construct is temporary, and a permanent commitment is necessary if the lasting of the subtle structure is desired for long periods of time.

One of the great advantages of working with constructs is their ability to being programmable. This means that a construct cannot only be molded in form at the desire of the practitioner, but can also have specific metaphysical functions, becoming a very dynamic structure. This is something that can be quite potent in a myriad of magickal workings. However, despite the advanced knowledge and training required for a more complex use of constructs, they also require a considerable amount of energy, not only to be created, but also to be programmed. If a structure becomes too big, highly complex or working very dynamically, it will consume a considerable amount of energy, which will have to be fueled by the practitioner alone with his own precious vital energy.

Constructs are very efficient for metaphysical protection in the subtle realms, and can be plugged into all sorts of physical objects, from doorknobs to full windows and even walls. They can be programmed to work as filters, letting pass the energies you want and blocking the undesired energies or beings from entering your own protected space, or they can even behave as true enforced shields, blocking anything from passing through. Obviously, the more intense and effective the construct needs to be, the higher quantity of your own energy it will need to consume. So, it isn't always easy to achieve the balance between an effective and functional construct, and its energy fueling level. However, small constructs without a very dynamic functioning can be far more easily created and maintained, and are a common practice among vampires.

Wanding

Wanding is an art created and developed by the Elders. In the Sep Tepy, the Asetians started specializing in the art of wandcrafting and their metaphysical applications. First, it was developed as an advanced spiritual tool to be used in more complex metaphysical practices along with the even more ancient talismanic technology and servitor creation. But soon its appliances would come out of the temples as a result of the need to create a powerful magickal weapon that would deliver a massively advantage in terms of metaphysical warfare. Its usage, not as a weapon, lingered and evolved, with the wands becoming great tools in other metaphysical disciplines that would benefit from such a precise and intense energy amplification device. It was not long since humans started mimicking the Asetian techniques and using wands in their own metaphysical practices as well, some learning its mastery and dedicating their entire lives to its research and perfecting the techniques, although none wielding a wand with the same skill and ability as an Asetian, with their inborn wanding skill from the ancient times. In time, those practices became more secret and the related techniques confined to closed circles of occult study, even among human practitioners. This led to an unavailability of the information to many people interested in learning the use of a wand as a magickal tool, and eventually ended up creating a new application of the tool to those who knew not how to use it – it became a tool only for the focus of Will in ritual magick. Given enough time, this tool gained popularity and users, and the use of a wand in ritual and other approaches in traditional witchcraft became a common practice until our days. Actually, these variants of wand usage, allied to the secrecy and elitism of the traditional wanding, became so popular and widespread that today it is very easy to find information concerning the ritualistic use of wands in ceremonial magick, but quite hard to locate valuable information for its use in direct energy manipulation unless the practitioner is bounded to one of the closed magickal circles that possesses the knowledge of the ancients, like the Order of Aset Ka. Today the practice of wanding is very restricted and only available to the elites of the occult society, but still a common use among these sects. It remains the weapon of choice for the modern metaphysical wars, wielded among the most diversified range of beings, from vampires to humans and otherkin.

When the subject is a wand, sometimes the concept of a *core* comes to the discussion. The core, or kernel, is commonly related to a substance or material that can be used in the center of a wood wand. The used material can range from animal feathers and fur to a mixing of mineral powder or other alchemical substances. The more effective core of this type is undoubtedly the proper mixing of mineral powders with different metaphysical properties, being a whole subject of study under the discipline of alchemy, which are commonly described as *last generation cores*. The core is expected to help in the amplification of the energy and its correct direction alongside the magickal tool. Unlike what is generally believed, cores are only used by beginners learning how to project energy from a wand. An advanced practitioner does not need a core; he even dislikes its use, since the core interferes with the vibration being projected by the secondary Shen of the hands into the wand, so it ultimately creates inherent noise in the transmission and conditions its intensity. However, to someone learning the basic skills of wanding, some variants of cores can be able to help in the projection, which although conditioning its use on a higher level, can propel the ignition of the technique used to project through a wand and help in achieving the steadiness of the beam of Ka, needed to properly wield a wand in a magickal sense.

The origins of the use of cores among humans are very easy to understand and correlate, having its historical roots in the traditional Asetian Wanding. Asetians tend not to rely on physical cores within their wands, but they use the concept of core in their wanding discipline. This concept, however, applies differently if a wand is wood-based, or mineral-based. In an Asetian wood wand, the vampire uses his own tendrils, which he consciously projects inside the wand, making its subtle core and vastly improving its use and effectiveness. This was the true origin for the use of wand cores by human practitioners, which without tendrils in their aura, had to rely in a physical approach to something that vampires always did in a far subtler way. However, this concept varies greatly from the one used by Asetians in mineral wands. In here, the core is not an extension from the vampire's own energy, like in a wood wand, but a whole subtle entity is bounded to this magickal object, known as a servitor, which was already addressed in this chapter. The use of low servitors in these wands is the most common practice, since it can be more easily wielded by the practitioner and it is also far more easily created. Elders and other highly advanced practitioners, if in control of a royal servitor of their own, would use it in their mineral wand instead of a common low servitor, resulting in a formidable magickal object and a great vessel for their own noble servitor. Finally, cores can be a concept used in a third different approach, referring to the kind of amplification spell used in the wand attunement, and not related with any kind of real physical material used by the wand. This ancient concept, also very used by the Asetians, can be applied to both kinds of wands, and is usually known as *edge core*.

Planes of Existence

The ability from the vampire to wander freely between the subtle planes has been known throughout the centuries. An Elder vampire is a creature detached from the physical, a being of energy that roams the astral in a powerful way and interacts with these other planes almost as if it was his native realm. In these other planes of existence, the vampire has the power to shape-shift, assuming whatever form he wishes. It can be a wild animal, or simply another creature with a human-like appearance. That icon in the astral plane is completely under his conscious control and bound to his Will and power.

Being the astral an etheric place where the vampire is the lord and master, more than in the physical realm of mortals, the Asetians have long learned and developed the abilities to experience the different planes of existence, manipulate them and wield them at their Will. The mastery of those planes and learning how they interact is of considerable importance in the development of the vampire, equipping him with tools and techniques for other forms of magickal work, energy manipulation, personal accomplishment and development.

Although *astral* is the most common word used when referring to the subtle realms, in fact it is only one of the main layers composing the planes of existence. There are five main planes of existence in the subtle realm, each being highly complex and composed of other more secondary structures. Each of the five realms is very different from the other and obeys to different metaphysical rules because of the whole construct of reality from which it is made. They are not only different in the way they are formed, but also in the way they will react to your own presence and how energy behaves in that specific plane.

Physical

The lower plane is called the physical, and although it is formed also from a subtle reality where energy flows and can be interacted with, it shares its space with the material physical realm. It is the realm where the body resides and all the physical matter, but it is also full of energy that while in this plane behaves differently and obeys to its rules. It is also the most easily accessible plane of existence, and where most of the direct spells, incantations and applications of direct energy manipulation are used. For example, when a construct is made and attached to a door, it is really crafted and present in the physical realm of the subtle planes, however it is common to create a linked clone on the inner plane as well, so that the structure does not dissipate so easily. There are some who even go further, and create another clone in the astral, although it is not that common. Many people confuse the astral plane when they are just interacting with the actual subtle plane in the physical realm or their own inner plane of thought.

Inner

The inner plane is our own realm and kingdom. We are definitive rulers of that realm and it is crafted out of energy – thought – and bound to our own true Will. It is also the realm of the unconscious mind, and where our secrets and inner wanderings are kept. It is a wide space, built out of our vital energy alone, and full of constructs created by our own mind, from our dreams, wishes, thoughts and fears. It is a safe place to roam, even though it might not seem like it. But all creatures found there are just faces and aspects of ourselves and non-sentient beings created by our mind alone.

This is also the realm of dreams, where we go when we turn off the conscious mind and simply drift away to this place of dreams and nightmares. It is possible to master this realm and consciously control it, which is how we can shape, feel and control our own dreams. With proper training it is possible to gain complete awareness of the dreams and actually control them. These techniques lead to the practice of dreamwalking, that is an effective door to the superior realms of the astral plane, like a key to the outside of ourselves.

It is also this inner realm that is the target of oclumancy. When a vampire wants to hack into someone's mind, for control or mind reading, what he actually does is to extend an energy link from his Third Eye Shen and pierce it into the victim's Third Eye, the most direct door into the inner realm. There are variants of this technique that rely on the secondary Shen of the eyes that are also quite effective. Once bypassed the natural defenses of the victim, it is possible to draw information from this inner realm, reading his mind and thoughts – past and present – and even gaining access into the subconscious. Sometimes this technique can be useful in therapy, and it is enforced by the Asetians in some of those situations. The created link into the inner plane of someone else works both ways, which means that just like we can draw information, it is also possible to intentionally send data through it. This is the form of manipulation and control used by those who master the arts of oclumancy, and a very potent social tool.

For people that do not embrace Asetianism and follow some form of belief-based system, there are times when they try to fundament the possible inaccuracy of the planes of existence defined by the Asetians with a range of theories based on loose accounts of personal experiences. There are many people who relate having seen and experienced a multitude of different realms and planes of existence, with a very different structure than the ones we define, where they have faced countless situations and made breathtaking discoveries when, in fact, whether these *realities* have been created by their dogma or imagination, they simply just exist in one single realm – their very own inner plane.

Astral

The astral plane is the first true realm out of ourselves and where the physical cannot reach. It is the place where most of the disembodied creatures reside. Although this is the place of excellence for the beings that are not currently incarnated, and those who cannot incarnate at all, it is accessible to the incarnated as well. The native beings that can be found there are made out of energy; not having a physical body, they are in their own realm, which is a considerable advantage that should be taken in consideration when interacting with them.

The experiences and different techniques of astral travel are of common debate and knowledge, although what many times is described as an astral travel experience has, in fact, only been able to project the practitioner to the inner realm. The projection to the outside and into the astral is not as simple and does have some associated dangers unlike what is commonly defended. You can visually roam by your bedroom or home and still be in the inner realm, since it is all stored in your memory anyway. It is possible to come into contact with strange beings and come safely back to consciousness. After all, the creatures found in the inner realms are just our own creations, like it was already explained. However, the beings that can be found on the astral are not that easy going, and can even behave violently, which given the advantage of being in their native realm, can become quite dangerous for the untrained practitioner that would not be able to subdue them. Dangers apart, the projection to the astral realm and the roaming throughout its plane are rewarding experiences and a good asset for an aware vampire. When fully mastered, it can be used for attaining subtle covenants and metaphysical gatherings, as well as interacting with other beings, incarnated and disembodied. There have even been metaphysical wars battled in these realms of the astral, which although not very common, have proven to be quite potent.

Not only vampires and humans are able to jump into this realm, but also other kinds of creatures, like the royal Asetian servitors, that can freely roam the astral, mighty as any other being native to that realm. There are structures built out of energy on the astral plane, most of them non-definitive and in permanent disintegration, others quite solid and empowered by the mind and Will of many. Some of these structures are of major importance and are surrounded by very potent enchantments, energy shields and even guarding creatures, like the subtle Asetian Temples on these realms, not accessible to just about anyone.

The astral plane is also where some of the high magick spells and magick passes through. Many people fail at high magick practices precisely because they are taken by their own ego, so the spell and energy are only projected to the inner plane and not into the astral like it should.

In the end, the astral plane is a wide subtle reality not so easily accessible as it might seem, but nevertheless a realm full of energy, life and mysterious things to discover, learn and understand, whose mastery is certainly worthwhile.

Ethereal

The ethereal realm is a place very hard to reach. It dwells above the huge astral plane and just below the infinite and unreachable realms of the Divine. Most of the beings never actually skim the surface of the ethereal reality, but for those who do, deep knowledge awaits them. It is in the ethereal realm that the Akashic Records are stored and maintained, so it is a place of central importance for anyone deeply interested in past-life work and self-understanding. However, it is a place that is very complex to find and access, and reserved only for the strong-minded, with a great and conscious control of their inner Will. Again, many people who think they are accessing their past lives are actually just watching impressions produced by the unconscious mind. This happens because they are accessing the inner reality and not the two levels above ethereal plane. This simple detail also explains why so many people find past lives of historical importance, or just related with what they expected, with a direct parallel with their own expectations. All that is stored and easily accessible in the inner plane, so when they attempt at a regression, they will go directly to those records and not really into the Akashic Records in the ethereal, that are highly complex to access.

This is a plane that people do not know much about, since it can only be accessed in glimpses of highly meditative work and only by those with a considerable amount of experience, knowledge and spiritual growth. There are also beings residing in this realm, but they are far scarcer than in the level below, the astral, and typically more developed, strong and powerful.

Just like in the sacred Asetian Temples below, the Akashic Records also have their own guardians and keepers. Royal Asetian servitors are also able to reach this realm, being a major asset to anyone that wants a reliable insight into their long gone lives and also a very strong defense while roaming any of the subtle planes.

Divine

The divine is the superior and most inaccessible of all the planes of existence. It is the All, the One and the Infinite. This is the root realm, and its complete understanding is beyond what the human mind can conceive in their material, physical mind. It is the last layer of the subtle reality, the one that enters deeply into the infinite realms of the Duat – the land of the Gods. No incarnated beings are allowed there, so no one can actually project into it. When beings, like the Asetians, are capable of contacting a divine entity, it is the actual deity that passes to the inferior plane of the ethereal to allow that kind of connection to occur. So, this kind of interaction is always dependent on their part. It can happen for a divine being to go even further, and into the astral plane, but that is something extremely rare. In the astral plane is more likely to be found a subtle entity trying to pass by a divine being, than a true deity. The Asetians hold very special ways to come into contact with the divine Aset, but that sacred knowledge is to be left out of the decadent eyes of human kind.

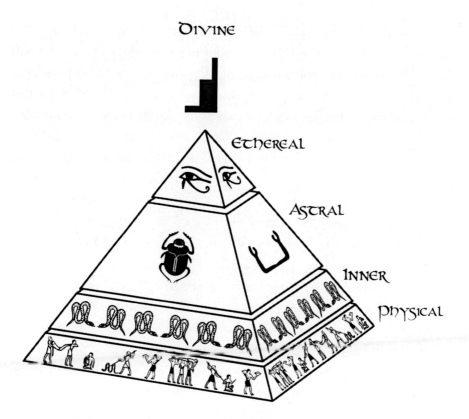

Astral Travel and Dreamwalking

The concepts of astral traveling and dreamwalking are different, although connected, and are related to the conscious use of the planes of existence, described before. Both dwell in the mastery of two different, but connected, realms – the astral and the inner, respectively.

Astral traveling implies the projection of the subtle body into the astral realm. There are several techniques to accomplish this and they will have different results for different people. Once in the astral, it is possible to interact with other beings; some disembodied creatures, native to that realm, and others that just like us are simply projected in the astral but have their own physical body as well. The soul is never truly disconnected from the physical body while incarnated, so the subtle body while on the astral is connected to the body by a subtle structure made out of energy and known as the *silver cord*. This silver cord allows a flow of energy in both ways and is permanently attached to both of the bodies – the subtle and the physical. If it is not present it is because we are dead and that would no longer be an astral travel but the way of life itself, since when the body dies, the soul is pushed into this realm, during the in-between stage. A disincarnated soul can also shift between other realms, and go as lower as the physical realm. These are the cases where people have experienced sightings of spirits and ghosts, which are merely beings from the other realities that came in contact with the subtle plane found on the physical realm, many times unintentionally and even unaware, others more sentient with their own intentions in mind. When on the astral, we come to contact with all these beings, so awareness and caution is advised once successfully projected. While roaming this realm, it is also common to discover a myriad of structures, which will be made out of energy, even when they do not look like so. The astral plane, being an immense reality, is composed by different layers. The lower ones have structures very similar to the ones found in the physical realm, because the mind and thought builds and reinforces those structures in the astral, which are permanently seen or thought of in everyday life. This lower layer of the astral also has many parallels with our own inner realm and both can interact very easily. In here it is easy to manipulate all the energy around us and shape the world to our taste. People create their own structures out there and sometimes even hold gatherings. However, the energy in these levels is very sparse and dissipates easily, so anything that you construct will not be there very soon, unless you constantly work on it. On the levels above, the energy gets denser and an exotic world of subtle existence can be found, from creatures to constructs that are not present around the physical and lower levels of the astral. It is in these lands where the Asetian Temples can be found, along with other sacred structures, and great adventures await those who dare entering these realms and discover all it has to offer.

Dreamwalking is more of an inner technique than properly an outer one. It relies on the possibility to consciously enter the inner reality without falling asleep, or to enter it while asleep and gain conscious control of it. By consciously accessing our inner plane, we gain the power to control it. This gives the possibility to explore your inner self, hidden reality and achieve a better understanding of your own life and identity. However, that is not the most common use for the dreamwalking techniques. Since the inner plane is so close and even entwined with the astral realm, this is a great door between both realities. By accessing your inner realm and getting control of it, it becomes possible to project out of this plane and into the astral. Since the inner is your own place of the subtle reality, it is possible, with Will alone, to shape a portal that would lead you out of it and into the realms above. The simple power of Will is enough in this situation, particularly because you are in a realm that is controlled by your mind. Once the use of that portal is mastered, it is even possible to invite people into your realm, instead of the other astral gatherings. You only need to reach out for someone in meditation or asleep, with him projected into his own inner realm or the astral, and once that connection is established, he just needs to enter through your portal and into your inner plane. Once there, it is possible for the other person to see and roam through the structures you created and your mind crafted, although that interpretation will always be highly dependent on their own unconscious mind that, once free from the physical plane and the typical function of an awake brain, will be widely active and influential on all your actions and thoughts. Just like two people would live the same dream differently, the same happens while in any of the subtle realms, manifesting different feels and interpretations to each experience. Also, this only should be done with someone that you fully trust, since it is possible for them to access glimpses of your own secrets, thoughts and life. What they have access to can be controlled, but it takes a bit of experience to master. Just remember you are inviting someone into your own mind, not just to your home.

Past Life Regression

The study and understanding of the past lives from the initiate represents a central backbone in the whole Asetian religion. Being a tradition that traces its origins so far back in time, much knowledge relies on past-life work. The Aset Ka is an Order whose members continuously come back, life after life, in a cycle of death and rebirth, so it is only natural that the mastery of past lives and the control of that cycle is part of the Order's inner secrets.

In the field of past life regressions, there are different techniques, that are used under different circumstances. Also, they work differently in each individual, making the research for the knowledge of a past life an extensive journey, not without peril. To gain insight into the knowledge of the long-lived past lives it is crucial to access the Akashic Records. These metaphysical registers are located in the ethereal realm of the subtle reality and represent the place where all the memories from past lives are stored. These records are not easily accessible or available, and are certainly well guarded, because their access is not expected while still incarnated, or by souls that are not spiritually developed. So, what is done in a true regression is bypassing those barriers and directly accessing the Akashic Records by projecting into the ethereal, or at least forging a working link to it. These are advanced techniques that are not easily mastered, and many people fail at regression attempts without even realizing it. The ego and the subconscious is the biggest rival of success in past-life work. Like it was explained in the subject about the planes of existence, it is very easy for the practitioner, while attempting at a regression, to simply jump into the inner plane or the astral realm, where he will be influenced by the unconscious mind and his own expectation and not really accessing the Akashic Records that reside one level above, in the ethereal reality. This results in a myriad of people with no notions at all about their past lives but thinking that they do. We live in an illusive world, where people gladly embrace delusion out of fear, ego and deceit. That is completely against self-evolution, and should never be enforced by an Asetian. Easy results can be misleading, especially when we are working with something so complex and subjective as the research of past lives.

The Asetians hold different techniques that allow them to achieve effective results in past-life work. However, those results are never accepted without further research or as an undeniable truth. They all require special validations according to the tradition of the Elders, not only through a process of triangulation, but also by other more ancient techniques of the craft. Asetianism is not a static tradition, so it is in permanent and eternal change and evolution, just like the initiate himself. And to this development, evolution and continuous increase of the knowledge behind the Asetian culture, the workings around past-life research and all the information gathered by these means, are of very high importance and useful tools for the whole tradition.

Vibrational High Magick

The field of Vibrational High Magick comprehends the most advanced techniques of direct energy manipulation. Some of these abilities are exclusively vampiric, and require powers that cannot be wielded by humans. Others require just a high level of energy mastery and control and can be practiced by virtually anyone with the proper metaphysical training lead by a master. Most of the techniques that fall under this category require an immense amount of energy to be effective and are capable of extraordinary results if properly mastered. The use of Vibrational High Magick allows for the vampire to control situations and energies other times chaotic or extensively dynamic and so ultimately uncontrollable, by relying on a massive use of energy projection, powerful Will control and other inner abilities sometimes exclusive to the Asetians. When properly wielded, an Asetian can manifest his power in incredibly rare, real-world situations, like controlling the weather and the elements at his favor, crowd manipulation and many others. The proper wield of an Asetian Servitor, wand and talismanic attunement, would also be considered Vibrational High Magick, although it surpasses energy manipulation alone.

Most of the techniques related with Vibrational High Magick embrace the most inner teachings and mysteries of the Aset Ka, and can only be practiced by a very experienced Asetian with the proper inner and outer tools well developed and mastered. Like most of the advanced Asetian knowledge and powers, these techniques are out of the spectrum of any publicly accessible work and are even kept apart from some of the initiates into the mysteries, not because of any knowledge control policy or elitism, but actually because of the high level of spiritual development and mastery required for practicing even the basics of these advanced techniques.

It is always important to keep in mind the high level of energy that all these techniques consume. It can easily let any vampire drained and exhausted if practiced without control and in a very short period of time, leaving him more vulnerable to attack. Viperines are clearly the ones that more easily master these techniques, since working with energy is something inborn and ultimately natural for them during their whole life and existence. But both of the other lineages, with the proper training and practice, can learn to apply the techniques and gain control of those advanced practices.

Metaphysical Tattooing

The mastery of metaphysical tattooing is a unique Asetian art. Since the beginning of the Asetian history, the practices of tattooing the soul are an integral part of their mystery tradition. The souls of the Asetians are not only fundamentally different from the ones found in humans, as they are also marked by a distinctive metaphysical sigil, engraved on the very core of each Asetian, in the substance of their soul. This procedure was created by Aset and Her three children – the Primordials – and has been kept a well-protected secret over the ages, a practice that only the Elders know how to perform.

An Asetian is an Asetian for the whole eternity. There is no turning back. Most of the Asetians that can be found nowadays have been born into the Asetian family long ago, given their immortality and sacred essence by an Elder in another life. This means that most of the Asetians are already born as Asetians in this current incarnation. In these situations, they already have their metaphysical tattoo at birth, also known as the Dark Mark, engraved on their soul. Only newborn Asetians, created in this current incarnation, need to be metaphysically tattooed with the Asetian sacred sigil.

What does also happen is that the Asetian might be given the opportunity to bear a physical Dark Mark in this incarnation, which means that he will earn a very special tattoo on the wrist, with one of the Asetian sacred sigils, a mark of their divine lineage and immortal powers. This tattoo is not merely a regular painting of the body's dermis; it is also followed by a metaphysical ritual, that is deeply connected with the practice of metaphysical tattooing that was used to create their soul's tattoo at the time of their own Dark Kiss – their Asetian birth.

The infamous Asetian Dark Marks, although a taboo in certain circles, are also a subject of much speculation and desire among others. They have influenced countless other traditions along the history, giving origin to practices of witchcraft that might look similar, although quite different in essence, as to practices and symbols found in myth and fiction.

All of this relies on the advanced techniques of metaphysical tattooing mastered by the Asetian Elders, that result in a sacred mark, that is more than just a symbol of their lineage, but a profound and integral part of their souls, a divine portion of their essence.

Subtle Surgery

The potential of the vampires as healers has already been addressed. The vampiric abilities when directed to vibrational medicine are quite astonishing, because of their inborn talent with energy manipulation, sensitivity and awareness. Interacting with energy is the Asetian way of life, so their talent in all of its different appliances comes only as something natural and inborn.

When it comes to vibrational medicine and all the variants of healing that involve energy, directly or indirectly, the discipline of subtle surgery is situated in the most complex and advanced techniques available. The techniques of subtle surgery are extensive and can be applied into many situations, from extracting subtle tumors to chirurgical removal of undesired energy links or malignant attachments. They rely mainly on the principal tools of any energy practitioner – the hands and the eyes – allied to the extension of tendrils in the case of a vampire. But there are also very useful instruments that are used in a subtle surgery procedure, which can range from a special attuned wand to specific types of minerals. There are even more modern tools that are sometimes used in the process of subtle surgery, like meters for the levels of Ka, energy inductors and breakers, vibration controllers and other instruments usually found in the most advanced laboratories of metaphysical research and development. Although a whole complexity of instruments and techniques exist at the disposal of a subtle surgeon, the effectiveness of his work and the reduction of parallel damage to a minimum, will depend greatly from his inborn ability and personal talent.

It is important to keep in mind that these techniques and instruments should never be used lightly. The whole process of subtle surgery can prove to be quite dangerous if done without the proper care, or if not executed by a well-experienced master trained in the arts of subtle medicine. The decision to submit yourself to a subtle surgery rarely should be the first option to take into consideration, not only because of the amount of risk involved in the procedure, but also because of the multitude of consequences that can result from the surgery itself. Unlike most of the energy-based healing techniques, a subtle surgery implies a considerable amount of time and care in the recovery, which should be closely followed by the subtle surgeon that has done the surgery.

The metaphysical sterilization of the environment is crucial to the proper procedure of a subtle surgery, whether we are talking about a minor or a major intervention. Like the use of skin and tissue in physical surgeries, it is possible and common procedure the use of the patient's own energy to close a wound, recreate damaged subtle structures or forge provisory channels for the energy to pass through. In most of the times, this is done using their own energy because of the dangers in rejection from an energy body that is fragile because of the surgical procedure, which might not accept energy with a different fingerprint in the most internal structures, especially when its defenses are severed. In situations of cauterization of wounds or removal of subtle structures, the rejection problem does not apply, but the recovery of the subtle body is considerably slower. However, one of the most complex and dangerous procedures in the practice of subtle surgery is any Shen intervention, because it represents a vital organ in the subtle system that is being the target of the whole intervention, and extreme caution should be taken, along with the proper metaphysical care.

Attunement and Initiation

The concepts of attunement and initiation are sometimes used indifferently, although they represent, in fact, distinctive methods and approaches of metaphysical work. Both practices are commonly associated with a ritualistic approach, although ritual is not a determinative factor in every situation, and can both be applied to many different circumstances, practices and traditions.

An attunement is a metaphysical practice that synchronizes a person, tool or object with a specific vibration. Although it regularly depends on advanced techniques, it is not such an extreme and important practice as the initiation. Attunement is regularly used in many energy-oriented practices, like the example of Reiki, where the three-level initiatory system is basically a form of attunement of the subtle body with the universal energy and the opening of the Shen Centers, which allows for a more clear and effective practice from the initiate. Some more advanced techniques are regularly used by the Asetians in the proper attunement of a magickal wand to be used for direct energy manipulation, in the balancing of the levels and stream of Ka flowing through the energy system, reestablishment of aura vibration and opening of the Shen Centers, synchronization of talismans or amulets with the essence of the Violet Flame, and many other applications.

An initiation is more of a life-changing procedure. It is an integral part of the life from anyone seriously into the magickal arts and the occult, marking the passage from one stage into the next, and is connected with very real changes, not only in a psychological sense but also in a metaphysical one, and sometimes even physical. Initiations are also common in a myriad of esoteric traditions and have been changed, developed and ultimately made useless by most of those same traditions along the centuries. The initiation rituals found in the eclectic Wicca and Christianity (in the form of baptism) are both examples of how can something sacred and transformational be changed into something inutile in a metaphysical sense. For the Asetians, the most sacred and important initiation is that of the Dark Kiss – the point of their birth to immortality. This is something that changes life itself, forever... But does not represent the only initiatory stage in the evolutionary life of an Asetian, and in most of the times, it is just the beginning. In Asetianism, initiations can only be done by experienced masters, and some of the most basilar forms of magickal initiation – like the Dark Kiss – is a gift that can only be conceded by an Asetian Elder.

The old days of the Asetian Empire might be a lost pleasant memory. The times of long gone formidable magick and epic battles might be over. But the Asetian bloodline lingers still. The Asetians are still here. We are still here.

We live in Secret. We live in Silence. And we live Forever…

Notes

1, page 52
Stoker, Bram. *Dracula.* (Archibald Constable and Company, 1892.)
Rice, Anne. *Interview With The Vampire.* (Alfred A. Knopf, 1976.)

2, page 63
The quantitative reference in terms of Ancient Egyptian godforms asserted in this paragraph are corroborated by the views of the Egyptologist Richard Wilkinson, expressed in the chapter *Egyptian Religion and the Gods* in his encyclopedic work *The Complete Gods and Goddesses of Ancient Egypt* (Thames & Hudson, 2003).

3, page 84
The *Kheperu Mantra* is also explored in an analogous approach in the literary work *The Passion of Isis and Osiris* (Ballantine Wellspring, 1995), by Jean Houston. The author discusses its metaphysical interpretations and symbolism in the chapter on *Hieroglyphic Thinking*, without correlating its interpretation with the transformation of the vampiric awakening.

4, page 93
The concept of Talismanic Technology and its applications by the Ancient Egyptians in their sacred temples, in the form of hieroglyphic writing, is addressed and developed by John Anthony West, Robert Bauval and Lon Milo DuQuette in the documentary series *Magical Egypt* (2006) on the episode *Illumination.*

5, page 102
Although similarities may be drawn between the archetypes used by Michelle Belanger in *The Psychic Vampire Codex* (Weiser, 2004) and the Asetian Lineages, true parallels should not be made because they represent very different metaphysical concepts. A Lineage from the Asetian Bloodline is a definitive condition of the soul. A purely spiritual concept and not something possible of choosing, being used as a ritualistic structure in House Kheperu, unlike what happens in the Order of Aset Ka where it represents a theological tenet.
The names of two Lineages, Guardians and Concubines, extensively used in Asetianism, were also referred by Michelle Belanger, as old names no longer used in her system.

6, page 152
The author Lon Milo DuQuette, in the chapter *The Evolution of Magical Formulae*, in his work *The Magick of Aleister Crowley* (Weiser, 2003), explains the strong implementation of the Osirian religious formula during the Aeon of Isis, from the Aleister Crowley's system – Thelema. The concepts within the Thelemic Aeons have a strong parallel with some of the Djehutys found in Asetianism, which the author addresses under a similar light.

7, page 183
The Egyptologist John Anthony West discusses the usage by the Ancient Egyptians of a subtle system of the soul and its parallels with the more recent Hindu system of Chakras, along with its relation with the overall architecture of the Temple of Luxor, on the episode *The Temple in Man* in his documentary series *Magical Egypt* (2006).
An extensive study of the Temple of Luxor's architecture and its correlations with the anatomy of the soul can be found in the classic literary work *Le Temple dans l'Homme* (Cairo - IFAO, 1949) from Schwaller de Lubicz, as a result from his 12 years research in Egypt, in an attempt to interpret the mathematical and symbolical implications within the sacred architecture present in the temple.

8, page 212
The examples of vampiric thought projection, described in this sentence, were represented in the Francis Ford Coppola's movie, *Bram Stoker's Dracula* (1992), in the scenes where the main vampire character – Dracula – induces Mina Murray to look at him, with his powers, when he is looking princely like. Inversely, he forces her not to notice him when he is in beast form.

APPENDICES

KEMETIC MAP
ANCIENT AND MODERN SITES

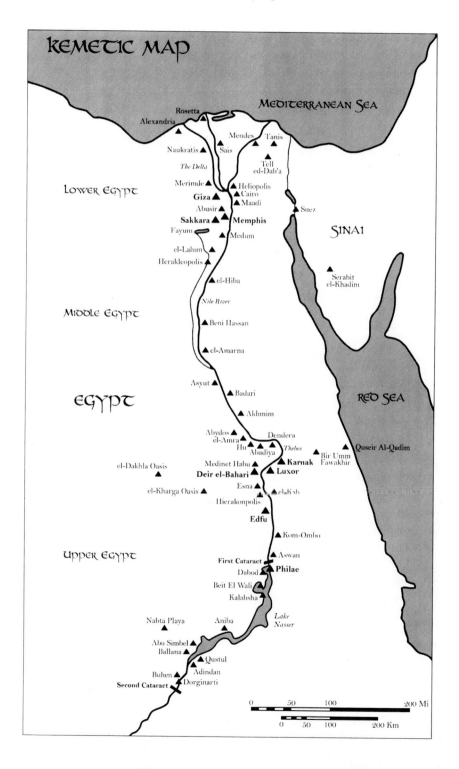

SHEN CENTERS MAP

BASIC SUBTLE ANATOMY

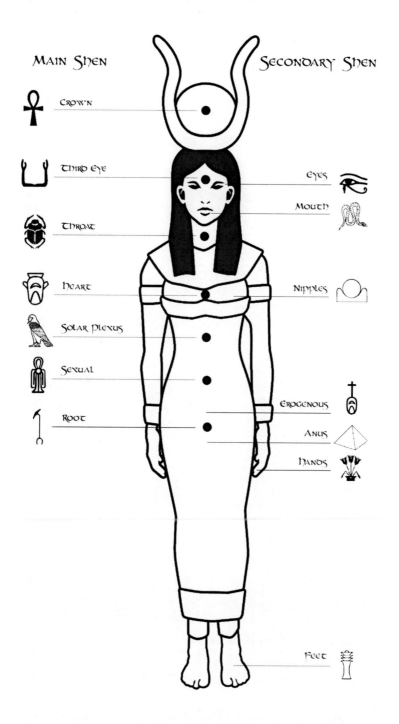

MAIN SHEN

SECONDARY SHEN

CROWN

THIRD EYE

EYES

MOUTH

THROAT

HEART

NIPPLES

SOLAR PLEXUS

SEXUAL

EROGENOUS

ROOT

ANUS

HANDS

FEET

SHEN SYSTEM TABLES
CHARACTERISTICS OF THE ENERGY CORES

Root Shen

Asetian Pillar	Was
Sanskrit	Muladhara
Location	Perineum
Color	Black or Red
Element	Earth
Functions	Strength, Survival, Instinct
Minerals	Ruby, Red Jasper, Obsidian, Black Tourmaline, Hematite
Physical	Spinal column, Anus, Rectum, Colon, Legs
Positive	Physical body, Material world, Grounding, Stability, Courage
Negative	Violence, Anger, Tension, Self-centered

Sexual Shen

Asetian Pillar	Tiet
Sanskrit	Svadhishthana
Location	Lower abdomen – above the bladder
Color	Orange
Element	Fire
Functions	Sexuality, Vitality, Energy
Minerals	Carnelian, Amber
Physical	Bladder, Genitals, Ovaries, Testicles, Kidneys, Suprarenal glands
Positive	Emotions, Desire, Pleasure, Sexuality, Surrender
Negative	Sexual problems, Confusion, Jealousy, Envy, Possession

Solar Plexus Shen

Asetian Pillar	Ba
Sanskrit	Manipura
Location	Below the chest
Color	Yellow
Element	Fire and Water
Functions	Nervous system, Digestive process, Metabolism, Emotions
Minerals	Citrine, Amber, Tiger's Eye
Physical	Stomach, Liver, Nervous system, Pancreas
Positive	Will, Authority, Energy, Self-control, Transformation
Negative	Anger, Fear, Paranoia, Depression, Hate, Digestive problems

Heart Shen

Asetian Pillar	Ib
Sanskrit	Anahata
Location	Center of the chest – Sternum
Color	Green
Element	Water
Functions	Blood, Life Force, Circulation
Minerals	Emerald, Green Tourmaline, Green Jade, Rose Quartz
Physical	Heart, Circulatory system, Arms, Hands, Lungs
Positive	Love, Forgiveness, Compassion, Understanding, Acceptance, Peace
Negative	Feeling repression, Unbalance, Heart problems, Lung problems

Throat Shen

Asetian Pillar	Khepri
Sanskrit	Vishuddha
Location	Throat
Color	Blue
Element	Air
Functions	Speech, Sound, Vibration, Communication, Creativity
Minerals	Turquoise, Lapis Lazuli
Physical	Thyroid, Throat, Mouth, Teeth
Positive	Spoken word, Communication
Negative	Speech, Communication problems, Ignorance

Third Eye Shen

Asetian Pillar	Ka
Sanskrit	Ajna
Location	Center of the forehead – between the eyebrows
Color	Indigo / Dark Blue
Element	Spirit
Functions	Psychic projection, Energy manipulation, Vision, Brain
Minerals	Lapis Lazuli, Sodalite
Physical	Eyes, Nose, Years
Positive	Intuition, Insight, Imagination, Clairvoyance, Will
Negative	Lack of concentration, Headaches, Tension, Eye problems, Bad dreams

Crown Shen

Asetian Pillar	Ankh
Sanskrit	Sahasrara
Location	Top of the head
Color	Violet
Element	Divinity
Functions	Connection with the Divine, Energy Source
Minerals	Amethyst, Diamond, Fluorite
Physical	Brain
Positive	Unification of the Higher Self and the Divine, Oneness, Infinite
Negative	Confusion, Depression, Lack of spirituality, Senility

SACRED NUMBERS
KEY ELEMENTARY ASETIAN NUMEROLOGY

2

Duality

The dual nature of energy present in everything. A symbol of the sexual polarity in the manifestation of energy itself. The completeness of opposites. Male and Female. Positive and Negative. Light and Dark.

3

Asetian Holy Trinity

The triple nature of the Asetian Trinity - the three Children of Aset, founders of the three lineages in the Asetian bloodline. Connected with the three stars of the Orion's belt, a sacred constellation to the Asetians, and intimately connected with their great *Giza Initiatory Temples*, commonly known as *The Pyramids*. Three also represents the cycle of evolution – Life, Death and Rebirth.

5

Manifestation

The planes of existence. Five is the number of the Universe and creational energy. Symbolizes the manifestations of the subtle reality. Air, Fire, Water, Earth and Spirit: the five-pointed star of the elemental quintessence.

7

Sacred Number

Seven is the number of Aset, connected with Her sacred daemons - the *Seven Scorpions*. In the Asetian tradition there are seven *Sacred Pillars* and seven energy centers of the soul - the Shen. Seven is the number of Immortality.

ASETIAN SIGIL
THE DARK MARK

KEMETIC ORDER OF ASET KA

The essence of Aset cannot be described by words or explained in books. The legacy that She left us surpasses religion, magick and power. The Aset Ka is that legacy. The true essence and secret behind the Aset Ka is far more than just a book, it is not found in manmade buildings or in objects, and is a whole lot more than just an occult order. The real mysteries that lie within the secrets of the Aset Ka are deeply concealed for more than 8000 years, and its doors will only open for those who prove worthy. Because for everybody else... we will never exist.

Lightning Source UK Ltd.
Milton Keynes UK
UKOW03f0615050617

302702UK00001B/266/P